THE GREAT ESCAPE FROM
STALAG LUFT III

THE GREAT ESCAPE FROM STALAG LUFT III

The Memoir of Jens Müller

Foreword by Jon Müller

Introduction by David Robertson,
cohost of *For You the War Is Over* podcast

LYONS
PRESS

Essex, Connecticut

An imprint of Globe Pequot, the trade division of
The Rowman & Littlefield Publishing Group, Inc.
4501 Forbes Blvd., Ste. 200
Lanham, MD 20706
www.rowman.com

Distributed by NATIONAL BOOK NETWORK

PUBLISHING HISTORY
Jens Müller's memoir of his escape from Stalag Luft III was first published in
Norwegian by Gyldendal Norsk Forlag (Oslo) in 1946 with the title *Tre Kom Tilbake*.
This is the first English-language edition and includes a plates section, a foreword
by Jon Müller, an introduction by David Robertson, and a historical note by Asgeir
Ueland.

British Library Cataloguing in Publication Information available

A previous edition of this book was cataloged by the Library of Congress under
LCCN 2018967075.

ISBN 978-1-4930-7791-5 (paperback)
ISBN 978-1-4930-7792-2 (ebook)

♾™ The paper used in this publication meets the minimum requirements of
American National Standard for Information Sciences—Permanence of Paper for
Printed Library Materials, ANSI/NISO Z39.48-1992.

Contents

Maps

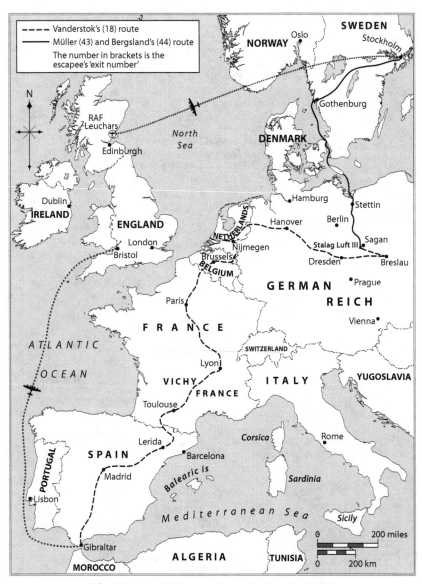

The Escapees' Routes from Stalag Luft III

Baltic Sea

Rügen

Stralsund

Slupsk

N

Stettin

Berlin

Poznań

P O L A N D

G E R M A N Y

Sagan
Stalag Luft III

Leipzig

Dresden

Breslau

C Z E C H O S L O V A K I A

Prague

0   80 miles

0   80 km

Location of Stalag Luft III

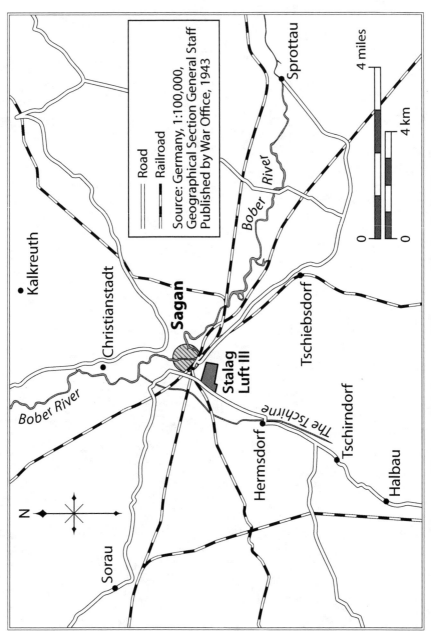

Transport Links around Sagan and Stalag Luft III

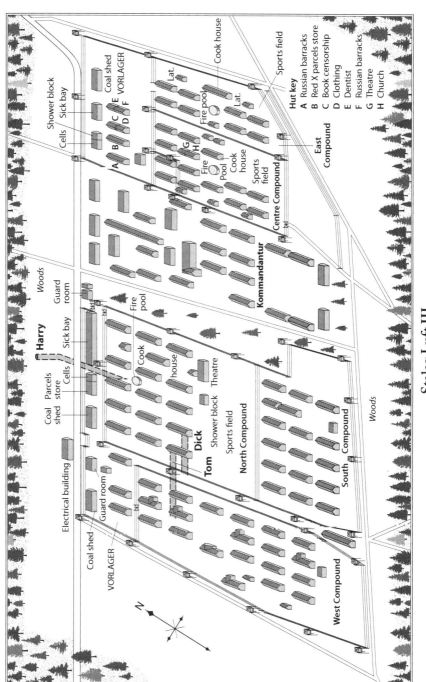

Stalag Luft III

Hut key

A Russian barracks
B Red X parcels store
C Book censorship
D Clothing
E Dentist
F Russian barracks
G Theatre
H Church

Shower block
Sick bay
Cells
Coal shed
VORLAGER

Lat.
Cook house
Fire pool
Lat.
Sports field

Fire Pool
Cook house
Sports field

East Compound

Centre Compound

Kommandantur

Woods
Guard room
Harry
Sick bay
Fire pool

Coal shed
Parcels store
Cells
Cook house
Dick
Theatre
Shower block
Sports field
North Compound
Tom

South Compound

Woods

Electrical building
Coal shed
Guard room
VORLAGER

West Compound

N

Foreword

I was nearly a teenager before I became curious about a small black-and-white drawing of a man in a dinghy, hanging on the wall in the dining room. The drawing was dark. It must have been nighttime and the dinghy was very small. I asked my father and he told me. It was always after dinner when he used to recount stories to my brother and me, and it was on a special occasion, when we were sitting around the table after finishing the meal, that I asked him to tell us about the dinghy.

So, he eventually told the story about the dinghy and the escape from the prison camp.

He also told the rest of his experiences, about training in Canada, flying Hurricanes and Spitfires and life after the escape at the end of the war. He never volunteered this information, he always had to be encouraged to tell it and at first it came in bits and pieces. It took some years to get the whole picture and then I read my father's book. I was fascinated.

My father was a quiet and modest person and it took me some time to realize that my father in the book and my father in person were the same. My father was not very talkative. When we did things together he just did it and explained to me without words.

I imagine that when he was escaping from Stalag III he was like that. Escaping without many words. Just doing it.

It must have been a very powerful force that drove all these men to escape from prison, knowing that if they were caught they could be killed. And they were all young. But the thought of freedom and victory drove them.

To make it possible to even plan that 250 men would escape from the camp, the organization behind the scenes must have been very strong. All kind of skills were needed to prepare the escape. ID papers had to made, clothing, money, maps – the list is long. The camp had thousands of prisoners; only 250 were planned to make the escape, but so many were asked to join the effort to make the escape possible. Those young men knew they would stay behind.

The two young Norwegians made it to freedom, with luck and also thanks to the skills of the men who had prepared everything for them to make it possible. Imagine being stopped by armed guards to have your ID papers checked. It worked … the papers were good.

Jon Müller

Introduction to the Paperback Edition

For many of us, it feels like The Great Escape has always been a part of our lives – whether from Paul Brickhill's classic book which first brought the story to a wider audience, the 1963 film which made it a worldwide legend, or the various tributes and pastiches which have filtered into pop culture over the years since.

In my case, I grew up with The Great Escape because I lived close to the hometown of one of 'the Fifty'. Alastair Donald Mackintosh 'Sandy' Gunn was born and raised in Auchterarder, a small provincial town in central Scotland, barely ten miles away from my own hometown of Perth.

I knew the name of Sandy Gunn as a small boy because my father, who lived through the Second World War himself, recalled vividly the sense of shock and horror which accompanied the announcement that the local doctor's son had been murdered by the Gestapo for his part in what became known as 'The Great Escape'.

Sandy Gunn was shot down over Müller's home country, Norway, in 1942 – he had been performing a reconnaissance mission monitoring the *Tirpitz* – and taken prisoner, after which he ended up in Stalag Luft III, became a digger on tunnel 'Harry', and was the sixty-eighth man out of the tunnel on the night of 24 March 1944. Making his way towards Sassnitz, he was recaptured barely twenty-five miles short of his target. Imprisoned in Görlitz, he was taken out and murdered on 6 April 1944, at just twenty-four years old.

Gunn was not one of the major characters of The Great Escape – he receives only a single, brief mention in Brickhill's book – but the idea that someone who took part in one of the most famous stories of the twentieth century was from a town only a short distance down the road stuck with me and inspired my continued love of Second World War prisoner-of-war escapes.

As a child, I avidly read books such as *The Wooden Horse*, *They Have Their Exits*, and *The Colditz Story*, to name but a few of the more famous escape accounts. There is both a consistency and a uniqueness to every prisoner-of-war escape story. Every escape is different in its own way, but each one begins with the same sudden shock of capture and incarceration. From actively fighting on the front line, within the blink of an eye the newly captured prisoner-of-war suddenly finds himself deprived of his freedom for an interminable period.

It is easy to forget that in contrast to criminals, who are convicted for a set period of time for their crimes, prisoners-of-war have neither committed a crime, nor do they know how long they will be imprisoned – but they lose their liberty just the same. Therefore, the initial shock of capture is followed by an almost instantaneous desire for freedom – at least among those who wish to escape.

We also often forget that the vast majority of prisoners-of-war had no desire to escape, content instead to sit out the remainder of the war in a camp far away from the bullets, bombs, and shells of the front line. Indeed, most preferred to pursue more 'respectable' pursuits such as theatre, sports, or studying for a qualification that would prepare them for life after the war. It was actually only a small minority who wanted to get involved in escapes. Even von Lindeiner, the commandant of Stalag Luft III at the time of The Great Escape, estimated that only around 15 percent of the camp population was ever involved in escape efforts.

While there was nothing wrong with pursuing other interests while in a prison camp, therein lies the monumental difference between Jens Müller and the vast majority of prisoners-of-war; he was one of the unique, elite few for whom prison camp life was unbearable, incarceration intolerable, and the boredom stultifying. Only escape, or at least the attempt to do so, was an acceptable pastime. Müller was not only willing to risk his life again in pursuit of escape, but also succeeded against enormous odds. This rarity only adds to his stature – and indeed that of this book, which will rightly take its place amongst a distinguished literary canon of prisoner-of-war escape stories.

Müller and those others who chose to attempt escape were not chasing the myth of the 'duty to escape' – a duty which did not exist in reality – but rather were in pursuit of the tales of derring-do which had punctuated and informed their own childhoods. For that is what prisoner-of-war escape stories are, tales of derring-do. Escape stories are performed by heroes enacting tales of adventure which most of us would never dream of doing ourselves, and fulfill that sense of excitement of which many of us dream, but few ever realise. That is why they remain so popular to this day.

Through these accounts, we get transported instantaneously to the breathlessly exciting moment when the mouth of the tunnel opens up beyond the perimeter wire and that first rush of free, fresh air cascades down, giving hope that this time, *this* attempt will be the escape which gets them home to their loved ones.

Furthermore, we get to follow our heroes through occupied Europe, where every interaction is a risk and every offer of help has its dangers. If we are especially lucky, we see them get to the relative safety of a neutral country, and from there onwards back to their homes.

That is why the memoir of Jens Müller is not just enjoyable to read, but a hugely important addition to the host of escape stories. Its place in the pantheon is secured by the fast-paced account of the escape itself, and by virtue of the important position it holds in the overall escape narrative.

The Great Escape is rightly remembered for many reasons. First, for the sheer scale of the undertaking made by the prisoners of Stalag Luft III. While much debate continues to rage around the rights and wrongs of whether the prisoners should have attempted an escape on this scale – six hundred were originally planned to escape through three tunnels – the seventy-six who did get out created enough of a hue and cry among their Nazi captors to ensure their deeds would be famous or, indeed, infamous.

Second, for the logistical organisation behind it. It was not just the digging of three enormous tunnels, but the dispersal of soil from those tunnels which needed to be organised. Furthermore, there was the coordination of maps, compasses, food, papers, clothing, travel, and forgeries, all of which were necessary for just one escaper – let alone seventy-six – to stand a chance of making it back home. And of course, who could forget the large-scale security organisation put in place by the prisoners to ensure none of this activity was ever discovered by the German guards?

Finally, The Great Escape is remembered for the brutal and cold-blooded retaliation from the Nazis. True, the Germans had made it clear that by this stage of the war – March 1944 – escape was no longer to be considered a 'sport', if indeed it ever had been. But in theory, the prisoners were still protected by the Geneva Convention, and should have at least been afforded the protections that were theirs by virtue of that pact. In short, if recaptured, they should reasonably have expected to be returned to their prison camp for a long stay in the 'Cooler'.

Instead, on the direct orders of Hitler himself, fifty extraordinarily brave men, for whom the war was never over, were shot in the back of the head in cold blood while relieving themselves on the side of the road.

Of the twenty-three who were recaptured, some were returned to Stalag Luft III, others were moved to Colditz, and seven were sent to Sachsenhausen Concentration Camp where, incredibly, four of them succeeded in escaping by tunnel again. (Unbelievably, despite the Nazis' track record, all of the Sachsenhausen escapers survived the war.)

Of the three prisoners who evaded recapture and made it home – Bram Vanderstok, Per Bergsland and Jens Müller – they have sadly become almost forgotten in the overall story of The Great Escape. And yet, that was the whole point in the first place: to escape from Stalag Luft III, travel incognito through occupied Europe, and get back to the UK.

Müller's reflections, therefore, offer unique insight into one of the most famous stories of the Second World War. This is all the more true because only two of the escapees – Vanderstok and Müller – actually wrote about their experiences. This book, therefore, constitutes 50 percent of the writings by someone who escaped and got home in the single most famous escape of all time. Much has been written about the escape itself, and the incredible organisation which underpinned the escape efforts. Yet more has been written about those who tried and, sadly, failed in their escape from Stalag Luft III (in particular about the great mastermind himself, Roger Bushell).

The insights provided by this account should therefore be treasured, not just by those of us who study escape both as an art and as a science, but by everyone who finds value in the story of courage, perseverance, loss, success, and sadness that is The Great Escape.

Müller's memoir is just one man's account, contained within the overall story, but it is a fascinating illustration which exemplifies the wider picture and, by virtue of what and who it represents, gives us a unique insight into the men who never had a chance to write their own account of the biggest adventure of their lives: The Great Escape.

David Robertson
cohost of For You the War Is Over *podcast*

Historical Note

Ask any Norwegian who Jens Müller was, and I am sure that most would reply: I don't know. Somehow Norwegian fighter pilots have not entered the Norwegian pantheon of wartime heroes. The reason is, I suppose, that they were never involved in any actual combat in Norway during the five years that the country was occupied, whereas other squadrons such as 333 Squadron who flew transport missions did. During the last decades Norwegian war memories have mainly highlighted the Norwegian Company of the SOE, the commandos of No. 10 Commando, the home front, and increasingly more marginal groups such as the communist resistance groups, Norwegians who served in the SS, and, through popular literature, the merchant navy.

Although the journalist Cato Guhnfeldt has produced an impressive seven richly illustrated volumes called *Spitfire Saga*, which chronicle the Norwegian pilots almost on a day-to-day basis, most of the fighter pilots remain rather obscure in the popular memory of the war beyond the air force enthusiast. Jens Müller's book *Tre kom tilbake* (Three returned) was originally published in 1946. It has to my knowledge never been reprinted in Norway (though an anniversary edition is rumoured for 2019). But there has been a steady release of memoirs from the Norwegian fighter pilots of the 331 and 332 Squadrons since the war. Most of these are informative, but one would be hard pushed to point to a definitive masterpiece of the genre released in Norway. Müller's book is important because it was the first, and because of the incredible story of his successful escape from Stalag Luft III on Friday 24 March 1944, which, thanks to Hollywood, has become known as the 'Great Escape'.

Müller was not bound for wartime glory from the outset, however. He came from a rather privileged family. Young Jens was born in 1917 in Shanghai, where his father, a civil engineer, built docks with armoured concrete in the Chinese port, which already had quite a reputation as one of the world's more mysterious seaport towns. His mother, Daisy Constance, was of English descent, but she was very much a part of the British colonial experience, and thus had some Chinese relatives. The Müllers had a second son, Nils, in 1921, and returned to Oslo the following year.

While he was still attending the Ris Gymnasium (roughly equivalent to a sixth-form college or grammar school), Jens became Norwegian champion in the 1,000-metre motorbike race in 1937, and also gained his pilot's licence the same year. During the summer of 1939 he headed for Switzerland to follow in his father's footsteps and become an engineer. Both Norway and Switzerland were neutral when the invasion of Poland triggered the Second World War in September 1939. Norway hoped to remain neutral, as it had been together with the rest of Scandinavia during the First World War, but on the morning of 9 April 1940 the Germans attacked both Denmark and Norway in what was called Operation Weserübung. While the Danes surrendered almost immediately, fighting continued in Norway, with aid from Britain, France and Poland, until the king and government left for Britain on board the cruiser HMS *Devonshire* on 7 June 1940.

Although a fledgling Norwegian Air Force existed before the war, as the Army and Navy Flying Corps, neither planes nor equipment were any match for the refurbished Luftwaffe. Most of the pilots from both the Navy and Army made their way over to Britain, most in fishing smacks, but some by air in those fatal months in 1940. These men became the backbone of the Norwegian squadrons within the RAF, but they were not the only ones.

After the invasion in April Müller and some of his fellow students made it to Britain via France by a merchant ship that sailed from Marseilles. And together with their fellow Norwegians they were sent to Canada for training in what became known as 'Little Norway', outside Toronto. This meant that the Norwegian pilots missed the Battle of Britain during the summer and autumn of 1940. When they started deploying back in the UK for the initial training on the Hurricanes in the summer of 1941 the Norwegians of 331 Squadron ended up being sent north to the Orkneys for their first mission. The Orcadian autumn and winter did not exactly raise morale, despite being similar to the weather back in Norway. A detachment was sent even further north to Sumburgh, in Shetland, in December. Jens Müller arrived there in February 1942, after narrowly escaping a training crash in Scotland. Most of the service in Shetland and Orkney consisted of scrambling after incoming German reconnaissance planes that flew in from Norway, but these scrambles did not lead to any German planes being downed. With the development of a sophisticated radar system, with stations at Orkney, Fair Isle, Sumburg and Saxa Voe, squadrons deployed in the north later in the war had an easier job in locating enemy planes and ships.

For the Norwegians, despite the north being closer to home, the main ambition was to be deployed down south in the Channel zone where all the action was. Three months after being deployed at Shetland, Müller and the 331 moved south to RAF North Weald near Epping and started flying regular missions into occupied Europe. It was on a mission to target shipping in the Channel that Müller was downed by a German plane and had to bail out, and it is more or less from that fatal day onwards that most of his story is based.

Unbeknown to the young Norwegian pilot, he was presumed dead after being shot down. His roommate Tarald Weisteen had the hard job of auctioning off Müller's belongings, which was the traditional way of raising some extra money for the dead man's family. Müller was not married at the time, but had a Canadian sweetheart, Alice Patricia Tayler, back in Montreal. The nature of the letters between her and her pilot boyfriend must have been of the intimate sort, because Weisteen burned all the letters to stop Müller's mother from seeing them. However, by 20 July 1942 news came that Müller had survived and had become a PoW. Via the Red Cross the squadron received a letter from him, asking them to take care of his money and to transfer £20 to Tayler in Canada so she could send him books and parcels. In general, Western pilots were treated well by the Germans and they had plenty of parcels and food during most of their captivity.

When Müller arrived at Stalag Luft III he soon became involved in the plans to break out of the camp. It seems to have been an ongoing endeavour, with many failed attempts, not unlike the cooler scenes from the 1963 Hollywood blockbuster – *The Great Escape*. However, there is otherwise little resemblance between the reality described by Hollywood and Müller's story.

The 1960s saw a boom in war movies, and in war movies set during the Second World War in particular. This was the decade of *The Great Escape*, *The Dirty Dozen*, *Battle of Britain*, *The Guns of Navarone*, *The Battle of the Bulge* and *Where Eagles Dare*, to name but a few. While *The Battle of Algiers* was set in the contemporary 1960s and was perhaps the most realistic in its approach, most of the Hollywood ones were either pure fiction – *Navarone* and *Where Eagles*

Dare may have been based on true stories but were heavily altered from the real events. Most of these war movies were catering for the young post-war generation that had not seen the carnage of the Second World War and – in the European context – did not have to go to war either. The Americans, however, became more and more involved in Vietnam as the decade went on, but that was still in the future when *The Great Escape* was released in 1963.

In the film we find a 'wild' American, Hilts (Steve McQueen), always desperate to escape, but to escape he needs his sophisticated British friends: McQueen played the young restless American, contrasting with the British officers as the cool, patient and calculated elder statesmen. Together they symbolize the special relationship that grew stronger during the Cold War. On top of that we have the hard-working Pole (Charles Bronson), who as a Westernized nationalist Pole, whose efforts echo the Soviet Stakhanov, labours his way to freedom, for himself and his Soviet-controlled country. Even the Germans are quite a tolerant bunch in the movie. Perhaps the most famous moment in the film is not the escape but Gordon Jackson's 'Thank you' as he attempts to board the bus to freedom.

In this context the film is much more about Europe in the 1960s than Europe during the Second World War. In reality there were not many Americans at Stalag Luft III at the time of the breakout, and the two Norwegians and one Dutchman who actually got away are hardly a part of the script. Suffice to say that Jens Müller really disliked the film.

In truth, not a single American escaped through tunnel 'Harry'. But in popular memory the great escape that took place seventy-five years ago has been formed by Hollywood as a great US–UK effort. That it not to say that Müller's book is without mistakes. He wrote it just after the war, about four years after being shot down. He recalls there being three squadrons in the air that day, but the records shows that only the 331 and the 222 were flying that particular mission in June. That is a rather good insight into the problems one faces with oral history. People remember things wrongly, and they have memories altered by things they have read later in life, and the longer the gap between the actual event and the story told, the higher the risk of adding things that did not occur. But I am convinced that Müller really thought that there were three squadrons flying that day. The moral is: always check the facts with the records.

Müller's book is in every sense a child of its time. It can be placed within the Norwegian heroic literature that was written in the first five to ten years after the war. Knut Haukelid's *Skis Against the Atom*, Max Manus's books and David Howarth's *The Shetland Bus*, all form part of this genre. Norway had been occupied for five years, and the country needed heroes, and books like Müller's fitted the bill. What makes it special is that it is a first-hand account of the spectacular events that happened three-quarters of a century ago. I will not put it up there among the great Second World War memoirs, but it makes good and almost effortless weekend or commuting reading.

Müller ended the war as an instructor but flew some transport missions when the war in Europe was all but won. He went on to become a civilian pilot, first for the Norwegian DNL, and later for Scandinavian Airlines Systems (SAS). He flew on the Far East and later transatlantic routes. When he returned to Canada after the great escape he found his sweetheart had married another man. Müller married a Norwegian air hostess, Liv Enger, in 1947, and retired in 1977. He died in 1999.

Although Müller was an avid motorcycle rider in pre-war Norway, one should be aware that the Hollywood movie's final scene with McQueen heading for the Swiss border is pure fiction. But readers of this book will not be disappointed by the back streets of cities in occupied Poland – sometimes the true escape routes are stranger than fiction.

Asgeir Ueland
Sandnes, Norway, September 2018

ESCAPE FROM STALAG LUFT III

Shot Down!

In the low height where we flew it was hot, disagreeably so. Drops of sweat kept dripping down my chest. Flying eastwards, facing the rising sun, did not help matters. We had left the English coast, and the North Sea lay in front of us like a hazy mirror. It was difficult to register height over this mirror-like surface with the sunlight shining on everything one looked at. I had to gaze fixedly at the sea so as not to fly right into it.

I was surely not the only one wishing we could have flown higher that morning, but if we increased our height by fifteen to twenty metres, German radar would register us and give us away. 'As low as possible over the water until the goal is in sight, and ascend only just before attack starts' was the flight order. There was one advantage to having the sun overhead – one had at least a fair chance of sighting enemy attackers if they came along. 'Look out for the Hun in the sun' was a golden rule. Both Allied and German fighter planes attacked preferably with the sun at the back of them. They could then make surprise attacks.

I looked for the other squadron planes. I myself was quite at the rear, in the left row of four planes, and had all the other eleven in front of me on my right. Now they had dispersed slightly while over the sea. It wasn't so very strenuous, flying in open formation, and one avoided getting into the whirl of slipstream from propellers in front. To my right, so close that I could distinguish his features despite oxygen mask and helmet, was Helge.* Next to him was Anton, who always flew steadily and smoothly. I allowed my eyes to wander further until they saw the other squadrons in the wing. They were a long way off, one to the right, the other to the left. So far off that they looked like two swarms of mosquitoes. Twelve mosquitoes in each. It was a safe feeling having so many friends so near. It would have been fun to chat over the wireless, but this was no trial flight. 'Radio silence until broken by wing-commander giving fighting orders.' One had to be content with one's own thoughts.

For at least the tenth time I mentally reviewed the instructions for the flight, as they had been given by the wing-commander in the dispersal room that same morning just before we took off from the airfield north of London:

---

* Lieutenant Helge Sognnæs and Lieutenant Anton Christian Hagerup. Sognnæs was killed in a dogfight over the Netherlands in June 1943. Hagerup became a Mosquito pilot and was killed by German flak over Sogn og Fjordande, Norway, the same month as Sognnæs.

'The Wing starts at 0900 hours, in the following order: –
222 Squadron which I lead, starts first. Then follows 331
Squadron (Norwegian) as No. 2, and lastly 124 Squadron.
We join on the way out. I keep to the right with 222. 331 in
the middle, and 124 on the left flank.*

'The target is ships running along the Belgian and
Dutch coasts. We must also reckon on some ships lying
close to land, and the attack must be made quite suddenly
so as not to give the land batteries a chance to get going.
We therefore fly at tree-top level as soon as we take off
and keep as low as possible during our flight over. We can
expect to find many ships in the mouth of the Scheldt. The
first one who sights a ship breaks radio silence and gives
me the position. If it is worthwhile attacking I will give
orders for preparations. 222 and 331 will do the firing, and
will therefore first continue along the coastline out of reach
of the land batteries while climbing and turning round
into position for their attack. Meanwhile 124 ascends
and circles seaward of the goal in order to gain sufficient
height to take care of enemy fighters if they appear. 222
shoots first, then 331, four planes at a time.

'Stick together afterwards and set course straight for
home. It isn't very likely the Germans will have time to

---

* The mission, 'Fighter Roadstead', took place on Friday 19 June
1942 and started from the air base at North Weald just outside
Epping. According to Cato Guhnfeldt's *Spitfire Saga* there were
two squadrons flying the mission, the Norwegian No. 331 and
the British No. 222. See Guhnfeldt, *Spitfire Saga Vol. II* (Wings,
2009), p. 74 (in Norwegian, but with English summaries).

get up before or during the attack, but on our way home we can expect anything. You must be ready in half an hour. Keep an eye on me. When I start my motor, do the same thing. One squadron starts at a time. Well, that should be all. Good luck!'

I could still hear his voice and see the overcrowded room, airmen in yellow life vests, maps on the wall, the blackboard with our routes drawn on it, the rays of sun through cigarette smoke. Then the usual wait before starting, the chat with mechanics about wind and weather.

It was unbelievable that I was sitting in a Spitfire on my way to fight the Germans. A year ago I was in Switzerland, waiting and waiting for a permit to travel through France to Bordeaux.* Then across the Atlantic on a freighter. The ship was an old tramp which ploughed its way laboriously through the waves. It had a crack midships. I used to stand and watch that crack. On wavetops it expanded. In the valleys it almost closed. The *Lista*† managed to make the crossing in fourteen days.

It was hot in New York, but not as hot as my plane was just now. Surely the motor wasn't getting hot? No, the

---

* Jens Müller began studying engineering in Zurich, Switzerland in the autumn of 1939, which almost coincided with the outbreak of the Second World War. As both Switzerland and Norway were neutral at the time, he remained a student until the German invasion of Norway on 8 April 1940. Then he made his way to England via Bordeaux.

† DS *Lista* sailed on 7 July 1940, possibly from Liverpool, and arrived in New York on 22 July. The ship sailed many convoys and survived the war. See www.warsailors.com.

instruments showed everything normal. The Rolls-Royce engine droned monotonously, reassuringly.

The weather was almost too fine. I would rather there had been clouds to hide behind when our machine guns were out of ammunition. At the beginning of the war German Focke-Wulf fighter planes made better speed than our Spitfires. This difference was corrected later on. Incidentally, last year I didn't believe that a Spitfire could sink a ship; I hadn't even heard of a 20-millimetre canon.

What's that over there with only chimneys and masts above the water? A wrecked ship. It must be shallow in these parts. We must be near land. The time? Fifteen minutes since we started. The trip over would take twenty to twenty-five minutes. I can see another wreck just below and to the side of us. A big fellow, probably a 7,000-tonner.

Suddenly I hear the wing-commander's voice on the radio: – 'I think we have land over there, two o'clock.'*

Convenient, this clock dial system: – the plane is in the centre of a horizontal watch dial, with twelve o'clock right in front. Three o'clock would then be straight to the right, six o'clock directly behind and nine to the left. I looked in the direction of two o'clock. Quite right, over there is the sandy beach along the coast. Green trees further off.

The wireless again: 'I think we'll follow the coastline at this distance.'

---

* Wing-Commander Francis David Stephen Scott-Malden. He was given command over North Weald Wing in March 1942, at only twenty-two years old. He retired from the RAF in 1966 as air vice-marshal. See: Guhnfeldt, *Spitfire Saga, Vol. II*, pp. 20–1.

We turned slightly off to the left and followed the coastline a good distance away. The Germans have surely spotted us by now but we are so far out and so low that it is hard for them to guess our intentions.

'Look out! There are some fishermen at half past eleven.' Our wingco is again the first to see. There were some twenty to twenty-five Dutch fishermen out for a catch. We flew over the smacks, almost touching their mast tops. Some of the fellows wave to us. Most of them are afraid of the Germans in the grey-coloured smack with the wireless mast. We have, worse luck, neither time nor ammunition to spare for the Germans just now. Perhaps on the return journey.

'There are some ships in there, two o'clock.' This time someone else had sharp eyes.

'Quite right. We'll have a go at them. They seem to be lying at anchor, three of them close to each other. They ought to be easy to get at.' Our wingco's voice sounded steady and clear. 'Cherry Squadron climb and turn. Cover us when we come out.'

I look to the left. Twelve mosquitoes climb towards the sky, get smaller and smaller, and fall behind as they turn outwards from us. It is 'Cherry Squadron' (124), which is to cover our return journey. We ourselves start climbing slowly, with 222, continuing along the coast and passing the western arm of the Scheldt estuary. Three ships lie at anchor close together under us. I try to remember as accurately as possible where the ships are before they disappear behind me. 'Look out – they're shooting at us from the island.' A voice in the radio. Sure enough, land batteries are trying to get at us in spite of the great distance. The black dots of smoke appear in the sky a long way off.

'We'll turn left. Piebald goes in last.' Wingco's clear voice. 'Piebald' is our Norwegian Squadron 331. We turn tail slowly towards land and make the turn before attacking. 222 cuts across us behind in the inner curve to take the lead. The turn is made and we can just catch a glimpse of the mouth of the estuary where our target lies.

We climb 2,000 metres and level out. The outline of our target grows distant as we approach. I release the safety catch on the trigger, turn on the light in the sights and give all engine instruments a last look-over. Squadron 222 is already diving in.

They open fire. The ships are hidden by the spray from shots hitting the water. Exploding shells flash on the sides and superstructure of the ships. The first four of my squadron follow on the heels of 222, then the next four. They are so close that I can see the empty cartridges being ejected under the wings from the firing guns. The largest ship is now giving out a great deal of smoke. Another one is listing badly.

Now it is my turn! I take good aim at the waterline of the largest ship. It is turbulent in the slipstream of the planes in front, and it's difficult to keep the sights steady. I open fire with canon first. The plane jerks. Shots hit the water short of the ship. I aim a little higher, and the flashes on the ship's side tell me that shells have hit their mark.

My speed increases in the dive. Distance decreases. It is time for machine guns. I fire and can hardly hear the guns go off, the noise from the canon drowns out the firing. But I can see the shots as they hit the water, and smash woodwork and other objects on the upper part of the ship. Suddenly my right gun stops and the recoil pulls the sights far off the target. I just have time to get the sights on target again and give a squirt with the guns before I have to pull up to clear the ship.

I climb away, the attack up to now having been successful. Not a shot to be heard from the boats, and only uncertain stray ones from land. Nothing more. This was too easy!

After the attack I find myself three or four hundred metres behind the others, and I open up to catch up with them. But they also seem in a hurry because the distance does not decrease much to speak of.

A voice calls out: 'Look out, Focke-Wulfs at nine o'clock.' Germans must have been attacking 222. I can see 331 in close formation on its way home.

'I see them,' sounded wingco's voice. 'Stick together and make for home!' He talks a little faster than usual.

There are still no enemy planes in sight. My engine is going full bore. I look around in every direction, mostly to the rear, where attacks usually come from. There! Right under me to the left is a Spitfire with a Focke-Wulf following it closely. Another Focke-Wulf appears! Neither of them have seen me. I see no others. Why not have a shot at one of those down there? I am at a safe distance and there ought to be quite a bit of ammunition left.

I turn round sharply and dive on the German. The guns work fine, when suddenly I see the tracer shots.

This means that my ammunition is almost used up. The guns work for a second or two, then stop – one after another.

I'm unarmed and quite helpless if anyone attacks. Best to get home while there is still time.

I swing around sharply, looking around for Germans. There's one! He is a long way off – a kilometre, perhaps further – and above me. The plane is silhouetted clearly against the sky, it is making straight for me. He may not have seen me. I alter course. The German also changes course. He has spotted me.

I gave full throttle a while ago and now only hope the motor will hold. I climb into some thin clouds, behind which I hope to hide. The clouds are too thin, more transparent than I thought.

The German is much closer. Every time I head into a bit of cloud the German comes out of the last one. Confound it! There's another German! And yet another! The first fellow must have used his radio.

Now they open fire, their shots go past, to one side of my plane. I have been expecting this for some minutes. I make a short sharp turn to get out of range of their fire, and succeed. I continue turning. It is now pointless to fly straight ahead, but the twists and turns slow me down a lot.

A few minutes later the Focke-Wulfs are so close that I have to make violent turns and manoeuvres to stay out of their fire. They are now close on my tail. All I can do is dodge and I do so as the sweat pours off me. The Germans use a lot of tracer ammunition. It is easy to see the smoke trails in the sunlight, and easy to dodge them.

Two other Germans join the party. Now there are five of them on my tail. It is only a question of time and I am done for. A couple of sharp reports right at the back of my backrest confirm this. The smell of gunpowder stings my nose. Then there is a loud explosion in my engine. A shell! The Rolls starts coughing, slows down, loses power, dies out.

I cannot believe that this must be the end of my journey. I can still hear my friends talking over the wireless.

A couple more shots rouse me. I dodge, pull the nose of the plane in order to slow down a bit. I turn the plane on to its back while I undo the safety straps and radio wires. Then open the hood of the cockpit (the bottom is up). I push the stick forwards and am thrown out of the plane.*

---

* According to the Norwegian squadron leader Helge Mehre the dogfights took place from sea level up to 1,500 feet, with most of the action taking place between 200 and 400 feet. The German planes, mostly Focke-Wulf 190s, came from an airbase in Woensdrecht in the Netherlands. The attack on the boats took place about a mile north of the Belgian town of Knokke. The RAF claimed three German planes shot down, but it was actually two lost for the Germans, while the Luftwaffe claimed to have shot down three RAF planes. Apart from Müller, the other Norwegian shot down was Karl Theodor Jacobsen, who was killed in action, and Sergeant Francis of 222 Squadron. Guhnfeldt, *Spitfire Saga, Vol. II*, pp. 75–6.

It is a pleasant feeling to free-fall. Everything is so still. Only a gentle swish, soft and agreeable. I fall towards the sea that lies calm and shining under me. I turn my head and see my plane dive with the bottom up. Then I pull the rip cord. Nothing happens for the first two seconds, then – a powerful jerk, and suddenly I find myself hanging with head up and feet down. Over me is the outstretched chalk-white parachute silhouetted against the blue summer sky.

I look around for my plane. A greenish white speck on the surface of the sea shows me where it has hit. I hear the sound of engines. From behind me come two of the victors. They circle round me for a while then turn their course for home.

I am still high up and have time to look about. Best to take my bearings while I can still see the coast. A good thing my map is in the heel of my boot. As far as I can see I'm two or three kilometres away from the coast and between the Dutch–Belgian border and Nieuwe Sluis, where our targets were. Between me and land is the fishing fleet we passed on our journey. Perhaps they can pick me up during the night. In the heat of the cockpit, I longed for a dip in the sea, but now I could do without it. It won't be long before I touch water. The safety catch is ready. It is not blowing very much but I have no experience of all this. You never knows if the chute will pull you under. It's best to get clear of it as soon as I touch water. Now the waves are clearly approaching, faster and faster. I swing a little and fall forwards as I touch the water. I duck under. Cold, green water. It is hard to swim up towards the sunlight with boots and battledress on. I am not quite free of the chute but my life vest helps and I am up at last. I struggle to get rid of strings and silk and gulp down lots of seawater. I am at last free of the chute and get hold of the string which is tied to the life vest. At the other end of the string, a metre away, floats the cushion I sat on in the plane. A rubber dinghy is tightly packed inside it. After some work I manage to open the cover and free the dinghy. Nothing is as easy as when they demonstrated the equipment at the station.

I find the bottle of carbon-dioxide and open the valve. The gas flows into the rubber dinghy and it soon takes shape. In a few seconds the bottle is empty and my dinghy is ready for me to enter. 'Enter here' is painted in large black letters on the yellow material. Easier said than done, since my wet clothes will not slide over the rubber material of the dinghy, but I manage to get on board somehow. The dinghy is full of water but I hardly notice.

The Rubber Dinghy

The time is nine thirty on 19 June 1942, a fine summer's morning. Lots of opportunity for speculation, if one's clothes had not been wet through and one's boat full of water. I had better start emptying the dinghy. Where was the bucket? It took me some time to remember that all the equipment for the rubber dinghy was fastened to the bottom of the cover for the dinghy. I started looking for the string by which the cover was attached to the dinghy and soon found it. I hauled in the cover with the kit.

First of all I took out a small canvas bucket, and in a few minutes my boat was almost dry inside. It leaked a bit. During the sixty-six hours I spent in it I always sat in a little water. Then I went through the rest of the equipment: a small air pump with which to keep the dinghy well inflated, a pair of oars made of canvas stretched over a frame of steel wire. (There were two loops to each oar: one put one's hand through one and grasped the next one. It was slow work paddling with these oars but they served their purpose.) Then there was a set of plugs to block any small leaks in the dinghy. A sea anchor, a thin mast and a signalling flag. Along the side of the boat a rolled-up cover was fastened, divided into two parts: one part was a flat piece which covered my legs up to the waist. The other part resembled a hood which could be drawn over one's head, it buttoned up in front and fastened on to the other part of the cover. If one closed the opening for the face one was well protected. With the sun shining right down on me it was too hot inside the hood so I gave up further experiments.

Plans for the immediate future started to take shape in my mind. If I kept away from land it was possible that Allied patrol planes would find me and notify one of our air-sea rescue boats. The question was how long I could keep away from land. The most important considerations were water and food. The breakfast I had had before starting would do me for one day. I thought of the demands of rowing home, westwards. It meant unaccustomed, strenuous work. No, my breakfast would do me at most only until early next morning. I had the flat tin box of emergency rations. I took it out of my inner jacket pocket, opened it and examined the contents: about two dozen tablets of concentrated food, one bar of chocolate, a packet of chewing gum, some sweets and a small bag containing six small white stimulant pills.* At a pinch all this could probably last six or seven days.

---

* Probably Benzedrine, the first drug that contained amphetamine.

The sun was now high in the sky and a slight breeze was blowing towards land. My jacket was almost dry, which helped to raise my spirits. I got out the oars and started slowly to row homewards. The sun and my watch showed me the direction. No land was to be seen, but it couldn't be far off. I paddled south-westwards to try to catch sight of the coastline. After paddling for an hour, treetops became visible on the horizon. That would do. I changed my course to follow the coastline. At first I just paddled, but after half an hour I noticed the dinghy hardly moved although I paddled evenly all the time. Then I started counting my strokes. One, two, three, four ... fifty-five, fifty-six ... three thousand and two, three thousand and three. Three thousand six hundred strokes were sufficient for the first hour. Then I rested for ten minutes. The next batch of strokes was three thousand. Then two thousand. Three lots of two thousand before I slowed down to one thousand between each rest. And I kept this going for the rest of the day.

After about five hours' paddling I realized that the tide would cause a strong current so near the coast. For some time I drifted eastwards in spite of my efforts to row in the opposite direction. And then there were hours when I felt as though I were in a motorboat sailing westwards.

Nothing happened that day. I just paddled. There was a slight chance that some fishermen who had seen me bail out would notify the Dutch underground movement. Perhaps they could fetch me by boat after nightfall. I had slowly given up hope of help from England. Of course air-sea rescue personnel made it a point of honour to pick up airmen who had fallen into the sea, but it was sometimes very dangerous work. Speedboats often ran up close to the French coast picking up men right under the noses of the Germans. But that was in the Channel. I was lying about 125 kilometres away from the English coast and only two kilometres from that of the enemy. No, the chances were very small, and I then understood that any rescue would have to be carried out by the Dutch or Belgian underground.

The sun sank lower and lower towards the horizon and it grew chilly so that I felt cold in spite of rowing. I pulled the cover over my legs. It helped. Then the sun set, large and red. Twilight crept up. The water which had been blue and glittering red was now green and dark. I went on paddling but felt like giving up for the night. I sat quite still looking at the lovely evening sky. Suddenly I heard the slight humming noise of a motor through the swish of the sea around me. Without giving it a thought I started paddling again. The sound came closer and I stopped. It was a plane! Many planes. They came from England. The flag! I got out the mast in a hurry, with the flag, and hoisted it. The sea dye! I threw overboard the small bag containing green powder which spread out on the water and left a broad phosphorous stripe on the water.

Far away on the horizon I could see four dots. It looked as though they were coming towards me! Spitfires evidently! The dots grew larger very quickly, and I could hear the noise of Rolls-Royce engines. If they continued on this course they could not help but see me! Now I could see the shape of the Spitfires clearly. They turned slightly, changed course and passed me low down over the water about a hundred metres away. They didn't see me!

I sat a long while staring at them as they disappeared northwards, the hum of the engines becoming weaker and weaker.*

I paddled two thousand more strokes before pulling the cover over my head and settling down to sleep. The night was clear and dark, and a sky full of glittering stars was the last thing I saw before falling asleep.

I woke up feeling cold. Looked at my watch. I had slept a couple of hours. By now there was quite a lot of water in the boat, and I had to bale it out. Then I rowed about two thousand strokes to get my blood circulating. There was a lighthouse far out towards the west sending its light over the horizon.

This time I slept until daylight. I could no longer see land, but the sun and my watch again directed my course. I blessed my waterproof watch. My arms were stiff from paddling the day before. The skin was worn off inside my elbows where they had rubbed against the edge of the boat while rowing. I hadn't noticed this before. During

---

* It could have been his own squadron, the 331, that conducted the search, but according to Guhnfeldt this remains an open question.

the night a hard crust had formed on the sores. At first it hurt a little but the saltwater softened the scab, and soon all was well.

I must have drifted far out on the wind and the tide during the night. I rowed westwards for three hours or more without sighting land. Only water everywhere. At 10 a.m. I at last glimpsed a pole far off. It must have been a buoy marking the way into the harbour. Land could not be far off. The pole soon came closer. The current must be strong. I soon caught sight of a smaller pole just beside the first one. Something white and cylindrical was attached to the taller one. It resembled the watchtower of a steamer. Of course! It was the masts of the sunken ship we had flown past yesterday. I paddled and drifted past it quickly. If I continued at this speed I would reach home in a few days. The mast tops disappeared behind me. Treetops showed again towards the south. This time I was drifting closer to the coastline, so close that I could see houses. They disappeared as I sank into the valleys between waves. I could clearly see a windmill when I was on top of a crest.

I began to feel a bit weary. I had not eaten anything since breakfast yesterday and by now there probably was not much left of that. Strange to say I didn't feel so very hungry. And I was not at all thirsty. But I ate four or five of the food tablets. They tasted of malt. I also ate one square of the chocolate. The chocolate was very satisfying, and to my astonishment the meal helped greatly. I had never before tried these concentrated food

Now they were coming right towards me. I quickly took out my flag and set the dinghy on the water. I hoped they would see it. I don't know why I made this effort. In any case I could not expect them to see me. They flew right over me. I waved my jacket and the flag, so I almost fell into the sea. I soon saw them grow smaller and smaller over the sea on their way home. A short while after, German fighter planes pursued them. Both the Boston planes and their pursuers were out of sight when I heard the Germans starting to attack.

The evening hours went by slowly. Twilight crept in. Then darkness. It grew chilly. I felt cold. I could not move about on the buoy without falling into the water. I was tired too, but could not sleep. I swallowed one of the six small white pills. A quarter of an hour later I felt its effect. I became wide awake. But I felt so cold my teeth chattered.

I got into the boat and started rowing outwards. The lighthouse was again working and helped me find my bearings. That and the Pole Star. I heard a feeble, strange sound. It grew louder and sounded like a ship's engine. It was evidently at this time of day that the Germans used their boats. The sound came closer. There must be more than one boat but I could see nothing. Only heard the noise, which came closer. Then I heard the sound of water washing against the bow. It was difficult to make out where the noise really came from. I gradually started to feel that I was in unsafe waters but thought it best to stay where I was. When the boats passed it sounded as though they were only ten or fifteen metres away, but the distance must have been greater as several minutes went by before waves from the bows reached me.

At one o'clock I started to row in to shore, and at three thirty was in shallow water and could hear waves washing over the sandy shore.

Dark clouds were gathering in the sky. I couldn't see many yards ahead of me. It helped a little each time the light from the lighthouse blinked over my head. Between each glimpse of light the night seemed impenetrable.

I swung my legs over the side of the boat and the water reached up to my knees when I stood. My legs felt wobbly. I pushed the boat away. It would surely drift off in the wind. I saw it move and disappear in the darkness. Now there was no way back – I would have to make my way past the German coast guards. Well, I hoped for the best, and waded towards land. The water must have supported my legs, for when I got on dry land I tottered and swayed like a drunk man. I could hardly control my steps. I swallowed another of the small white pills. The wooden shipwreck lay there in the dark but I did not need it to hide me.

I got down on all fours and crawled inland. Afraid of landmines, I crawled along very slowly, feeling my way with my hands. Later I realized this would not have helped me much. At first the sand was wet and hard. I heard only the sound of waves behind me. I crawled on further up the beach where the sand was drier. Then I lay still and listened.

I could make out sounds coming from inland which must be Germans talking to one another. Judging by the sound they must be quite close to me. I crawled on still further until I could hear the voices more clearly. They must be the crew of a machine-gun nest. For some time I crawled on my stomach parallel with the water's edge and heard the voices fade out behind me.

I heard new voices in front of me in the dark. A new position. I turned and crawled back again a little until I thought I was right in the middle between the positions. Then I turned once more inland and crawled slowly and quietly forwards. Soon I could hear soft voices on either side of me in the darkness. They seemed to be quite close and I tried to camouflage myself. I rolled about in the soft sand so that my damp uniform became covered with sand. I crawled on further and could now almost make out what they were saying. One German was evidently cleaning his rifle. I could hear the mechanism click.

The voices faded as I reached the barbed-wire fence. I could see the wire in the flashes from the lighthouse. There might be an alarm system in them, and I crept back and forth for some time before feeling safe. An hour and a half had now gone since I had seen the dinghy disappear.

It looked like an ordinary barricade, and I crawled under the lowest strand of barbed wire. It took me half an hour to get through this fence. It was about fifteen to twenty metres deep.

Behind the fence the sand was no longer even. There were little mounds here and there and small tufts of rushes. I lay quiet listening for a while. Couldn't hear a sound. I continued crawling on my belly until I got between the mounds, then crawled further on my hands and knees. Still no sound, only the noise of the waves at a distance behind me. The rushes were more plentiful now and grew higher. Here and there were low bushes. The possibilities for hiding were more promising and I crawled in between the bushes as often as I could. The mounds became higher. The bushes grew thicker and thicker. Quite often I lay still to listen. No life anywhere.

I came to the top of one mound and saw a barbed-wire barricade. I crawled alongside this, down in a dip between two mounds. This barricade was much thicker than the first one, more like a solid barbed-wire fence. There was no way through it. I had to climb over it. It creaked while I climbed it.

Once on the other side I stood a long while and listened. The bushes here were about the height of a man. Not a sound broke the stillness of the night. I could well be four or five hundred metres from the beach now and began to feel safe. I went on.

It was good to stretch oneself straight up among the tall bushes. The dunes also gave good shelter. I had to bend down a bit where the bushes were not so tall. I could hardly hear my footsteps in the soft sand. Soon I would come to some houses. Perhaps a farm. I knew the Dutch

I was then shown into a small side room. The door was locked and I was alone. In spite of everything I could not help liking the captain. He treated me with tact and thoughtfulness considering I was a prisoner of war. The manner in which he spoke to those under him showed that he was a good-hearted fellow. I must say the same for all those with whom I came in contact in the guardroom.

There were iron bars on the outside of the window in my room. No possibilities. I lay down on the bunk and slept until dinner was brought in. It consisted of a large portion of meat, potatoes and raw tomatoes. I ate most of it and went to sleep again until awakened by the door opening and the captain entering with a lieutenant and Feldwebel from the air force. They told me to dress. They were taking me elsewhere.

After saying goodbye to the captain, I was taken out to the courtyard to a motorcar and driven out of the camp and onto the main road. I tried to keep track of the direction in which we drove but we soon turned into some side streets so it was difficult. The guards said nothing. But we travelled mostly in a south-westerly direction, through Belgium and into France. We started at one o'clock, and now the weather was fine and the sun shone. After a couple of hours' driving, we had a puncture. Out of the car. The guards got out their pistols at once. The spare tyre was soon put on and our journey continued. At six o'clock we passed an aerodrome lying on the outskirts of a town. 'St Omer' was written on a sign at the border. I seemed to recognize the place as we had flown over it when on the lookout for German planes, and we were usually pursued by airmen from St Omer. They flew Focke-Wulf 190s.

We had just passed the sign when another tyre blew out. This time it had to be repaired at a garage. The driver found a bowing and scraping Frenchman who promised to repair the tyre. It would take an hour and a half. The lieutenant who had charge of me thought it best to take me to the mess at the aerodrome. We reached the gate in ten minutes and after some discussion with the guard obtained admittance. The first thing which struck me was the way the Germans camouflaged workshops, buildings and hangars. In England they used paint. Here large wooden frames were put up and covered with netting. Thus a hangar could resemble a haystack. Some smaller buildings looked like the outhouses on a farm. It was very effective at a distance.

The lieutenant took me into the mess, a new wooden building. The place was empty and we walked through it to the front of the house overlooking a courtyard. Six or seven German airmen with life vests and parachutes sat sunning themselves. The planes, Focke-Wulf 190s, were parked close by. Apart from them, the picture was practically the same as could be seen at any British fighter station. The pilots were quite young. They looked with curiosity at me and the guard and made room for us among them. Sandwiches were placed on the table. A large plateful. Also tea and cognac. They insisted upon my eating and drinking and assured me that there was more than enough food. Well, I didn't doubt that as they all looked well and as active airmen probably got first-rate rations. However, they talked so much about food and wine that I guessed they were afraid that Allied propaganda was saying that the German forces were almost starving.

The squadron commander was a quite young, fair-haired and lively fellow, one hundred per cent Nazi. He told me how much sport they did at his unit. They did sport all day. Then he started on politics. Talked on for a time. The conversation turned to flying and German planes, but I couldn't get much out of them. They asked me twice if I had joined the RAF in order to make money. They evidently wanted to make me angry. We agreed, however, that German airmen earned more than the Allied ones.

While we sat there asking about each other's equipment, planes were taking off and landing, all Focke-Wulf 190s. It looked as though this type of plane was difficult to land, as most of them swerved to one side on landing, which could also mean that German airmen were not well trained. Four machines were parked twenty-five metres from our table, but I got no chance to have a look at them. At last I asked outright if I could look into one of the cockpits. They laughed heartily at this, as I had expected them to.

Later they told me one thing before we left and that was that some days ago they had shot down two Spitfires at the mouth of the Scheldt. This gave me food for thought.*

---

* According to Guhnfeldt, there is no evidence that fighters from St Omer took part in the battle that led to Müller being shot down. One explanation could be that they had heard about it, or

The car was in order when we returned to the garage. Twenty minutes' driving brought us to our destination, a transit office for prisoners of the air force. Here again I had to fill in forms and there I did something regrettable. I gave them my family's address in Norway. My fear that something would happen to them through this luckily had no foundation, as I learned later. During the time I was a prisoner of war in Germany I corresponded regularly with my mother and brother at home.

When the forms were filled in they brought me a piece of sausage, bread and a lump of margarine and I was shown to a cell in the attic with a guard over me.

I lay on my bunk for a long time, thinking over the situation. It was strange that the Germans didn't seriously try to get something out of me, being as tired as I was then. One whole day had passed since my capture and as yet I had not really been cross-examined. If they had done this as soon as I was caught they might have been able to get something out of me. In England the Intelligence Department examined prisoners as soon as possible after they were caught, while they were still dazed after having been shot down. Thus they often divulged valuable information. Now, however, I felt quite refreshed and had had enough time to think over what and what not to say. Well, it was their affair and the longer they postponed the cross-examination the longer I would have to collect my thoughts.

---

that by pure coincidence some of the pilots had flown down from the Netherlands. See Guhnfeldt, *Spitfire Saga, Vol. II*, p. 85.

As far as I knew I was the first Norwegian in uniform whom they had shot down and made prisoner.* I therefore expected them to be very interested.

The door of my cell was open the whole night with a guard outside. On the street in front of the building the heavy footsteps of another guard could be heard. They echoed monotonously off the wall of the house opposite.

I soon fell asleep and awoke at dawn to find a German shaking me. 'Get up,' he said. Then, 'Follow me.'

The guards from our motor trip the day before were in the front room downstairs waiting for me, and the car was outside. After driving for five minutes we came to a railway station. I asked where we were going now. As expected, the answer was, 'Frankfurt am Main.'

On the platform I saw a number of German soldiers and French civilians. Some of them turned to look at us. At six o'clock the train arrived, chock-full of Germans – evidently on furlough, judging by their happy faces.

We got a compartment to ourselves, I and my guards, but the lieutenant had a job explaining it was 'occupied'. People looked at the empty seats, opened their mouths in protest, but saw my uniform, changed their minds and disappeared.

The train was a slow one and often stopped. Once it waited two hours at a station before continuing. I complained about the ventilation in the compartment.

---

* This seems to be correct, although some Norwegians had been killed in action and accidents previously.

The two guards looked at me, then at one another. I had to smile. They were afraid I would use a convenient moment to jump out of the window. But it was hot and uncomfortable so they finally opened the window. I got up and went to the window to get some air and could see that they had their hands on their pistols.

The train often went so slowly that one could have jumped out without hurting oneself very much. I looked back at the row of carriages on the train. German soldiers were hanging out of all the windows. I gave up the idea for the time being and sat down. It seemed that my guards were also on furlough and in taking the job of watching me would get two extra days' holiday. For this reason they were friendly to me. However, we did not talk much on the journey. The Feldwebel now and then tried to start up an argument, but was such a staunch Nazi that I was not interested. The lieutenant seemed to be more broad-minded, but he would not talk freely while his subordinate listened. So we sat staring at the passing landscape. Now and then we ate something. In the afternoon we came to a town where we had to change trains. We had a lot of time and the lieutenant took me to the soldiers' mess, where we got a plate of vegetable soup. The place was like the ones in England. There were rows of tables and benches, and behind a long table women in uniform were dishing out food. A throng of soldiers were coming and going, with kit and without. We sat there for three-quarters of an hour. There was evidently great difficulty in getting reserved seats on the train and the Feldwebel was put in charge of me while the lieutenant talked to the traffic authorities. I stood looking at the people coming and going on the platform. Once I heard someone whistling softly but distinctly: – 'There Will Always be an England'. I looked round but could not tell who it was among all the faces. A French porter stood a little apart, at the entrance to the street. Our eyes met. He looked round carefully, looked at me again and winked one eye. Just then the lieutenant came back.

We found the train and an empty compartment. Shortly afterwards the train left the station. The corridor was full of soldiers as before. The window in the compartment was open but my guards were too ready with their pistols for me to chance jumping out. I thought, probably as many had done before me and since, 'There will always be a chance to escape when I get to the prison camp.'

Had I known how small that chance would be and that it would be twenty-two months before I would get mine, I think I would have jumped, even against great odds.

In the evening we crossed the border and at sunset were journeying south through the Rhine Valley. Dusk had set in when we arrived at the station at Cologne. Not much of the town had been bombed yet. We had to change trains again and went into the restaurant. My arms started aching. They were bleeding and my uniform stuck to the sores. It annoyed me and I asked for a bandage. The lieutenant was very concerned and said he had no idea I had been wounded. I had not been: it was the rowing in the dinghy which had gradually scraped off the skin. All would be well if I could only have some plaster. He took me to a first-aid post and a nurse bandaged me nicely.

It was now quite dark; the blue lights in the halls and on the platforms made the people colourless. Only the restaurant was lit up. On the whole, civilians looked pleased and happy. We didn't stay there long, just managed to drink a glass of beer before the train left. The lieutenant said we were now on the last stage of our journey. Frankfurt am Main was our next stop. We arrived at six the next morning. The Feldwebel was going further. I said goodbye to him but he didn't answer, only scowled and left. The lieutenant who was going to take me to the camp led the way out of the station and to a tramcar, in which we travelled for a quarter of an hour before leaving the town. We went on further for about an hour, while I tried to remember the road we took. When we got off at the small station a Feldwebel stood there waiting for us. Papers were signed and I was officially given over to his charge. The lieutenant took the tramcar back to town and my new guardian showed me the way to the prison camp.

In Camp

We went through a lovely landscape, broad valleys, fir-covered hills and green fields, where whitewashed farmhouses stood. We walked on a path across some fields and through a small forest. The camp soon became visible among the trees. It lay at the foot of a hill and from the path looked like a large farmhouse. I mentioned this to the Feldwebel, who explained that the houses we saw were a model farm just near the camp. We could not see the huts yet. The farm was run by young girls from town and other outskirts.

The Feldwebel pointed to a large house. 'Headquarters,' he said in good English, and I asked where he had learned it. Well, he had spent a couple of years in England just before the war.

'How did you like Canada?' he asked.

'I don't know,' I said, 'I have never been there.'

'Is that so? I thought all Norwegians were trained in Canada.' He showed me an American magazine he had, with pictures from Toronto. I said nothing, only thought it best to be on my guard.

We came to a courtyard overgrown with grass between low, long huts. Most of them had iron bars on the windows. The German led the way into one of the huts and after a great deal of talk with the guard I was taken in by them both. A long corridor leading into cells on either side ran right through the huts. The doors looked strong enough. We stopped at one of them. The guard opened the door and I was shown in.

'And now give me your clothes, please.'

'What?' I said.

'Kindly give us your clothes, we are going to search you.'

When I protested, explaining that I had already been searched, they said they regretted having to bother me again to take my clothes off. Well, there was nothing else to do but take off my uniform, keeping on underwear and socks. I had a small packet containing French money hidden in my socks. This money had been in the tin box with my emergency rations. They were not satisfied merely to get my clothes but examined my body all over on the outside and almost inside too! And found the money of course. 'Aha,' they said, and went away.

I looked around the cell. It seemed to be three by two metres. The furniture consisted of a bed, a stool and a table. On the bed was a mattress filled with wood shavings. In the table drawer I found a spoon, a fork and a wooden knife. The window could only be opened with a special key. A small opening over the window was nailed down but I got it open. Through the iron bars the view from the window was beautiful. The bars were very strong. I wondered if I would spend the rest of my days in this cell.

Then I remembered what they had told us in England about Durchgangslager Luft, Frankfurt am Main. Three or four Englishmen had managed to escape from Germany after having been in the camp.* Afterwards they had visited most of the RAF stations in England recounting their experiences. They had said something about a prisoner being kept in a cell all alone until the Intelligence Department was through with him. Only then was he let loose among the other prisoners.

I tried to remember all I had been told, about the microphone in the ceiling, about pleasant Germans and angry ones, about so-called Red Cross representatives and about Germans dressed as Englishmen. Germans could think of many things. Well, I was prepared for most of them. I wondered what time it was as my watch had been taken from me. A key turned in the keyhole and a Feldwebel entered. He had my clothes on his arm. He seemed a nice fellow, fair hair, blue eyes – cold eyes.

---

* The camp was known as Dulag Luft, and was situated near the town of Oberursel, near Frankfurt. The escape attempt took place during late spring of 1941, but all escapees were captured, and hence it might be a story Müller heard about during his stay at Stalag Luft III.

I didn't like them. His uniform was well pressed. He smiled broadly, 'Good morning.'

I was surprised. He had quite an English voice and intonation, nothing German about his accent. He went on introducing himself and apologized for having kept my clothes and belongings for so long. I must have seemed uninterested because while he was talking I was trying to detect something German in his accent. But I couldn't find anything. He sat down on the stool and kindly offered me a cigarette. I thanked him and took one. When I asked where he had learned English he willingly told me he had lived in England for many years. He had also been to America. He asked where I came from. 'Oslo, Norway,' I told him.

We chatted a while about different things and the German tried perceptibly to be entertaining and charming. He then pulled out a form. As he came around to the table to place the form before me I noticed a white band on his arm with a red cross on it. 'Aha,' I thought. 'Here is the Red Cross form we were warned against in England.' I read what was on it with curiosity. As expected, it started with the usual innocent questions. Gradually they changed from only personal (name, age, birthplace, etc.) to technical and tactical questions (station, squadron, leader's name, number of planes, etc.) I filled out what I thought fit and said I was sorry I could not answer the rest of them.

The German first explained how necessary it was to answer all the questions. Necessary for informing authorities and relatives that I was taken prisoner. When I still refused his face grew dark. He said that if I didn't fill out the form fully they had no other way of knowing if I really belonged to the RAF. I could be a spy for all they knew. Did I know what that meant? Yes, I knew. I still refused to complete the form.

At this point the German lost patience. He snatched up the form and left the cell. He must have gone through the same farce a hundred times, always with the same result. But he had played his part well, so well that he would perhaps bluff some if they had not been briefed and warned.

It was a relief to hear the door slam behind the German. I pulled at a rope hanging beside the door and expected a bell to ring which would bring the guard. Not a sound came from it. I knocked on the door and waited for the guard to come. No one came. Then I banged on the door. That helped. Heavy footsteps clanked along the corridor, the door opened and a soldier looked at me in astonishment.

'Could I have a book to read?' I asked. 'And I want to wash myself.'

'Yes, yes, just wait,' was the reply. The German closed the door and his footsteps died away down the corridor. I lay on the bed and waited. One hour passed before footsteps were heard. The door opened and two soldiers entered with soup and plates in a basket. They placed a plate of soup and two slices of bread on the table and disappeared, wishing me 'Good appetite'. Yes, my appetite was OK, but the thin soup and the two pieces of bread didn't help much. I lay down on the bed and slept.

I heard the bolts being drawn back on the door and sat up. A German major entered the room.

'Please, don't get up,' were his first words. I preferred to get up. He sat down and asked me to do the same. He offered me a cigarette. I waited anxiously for what was coming. We had been told so much about this camp and German methods of obtaining information that I expected to have military secrets pumped out of me without even knowing it. All the Germans I had hitherto come in contact with had used simple, direct methods for interrogation, methods which were easy to counter.

I expected this major to give me trouble – but his methods were as stereotyped as the others. I made use of his efforts to be friendly to ask him for some reading matter and toilet articles. There was of course nothing he would rather do than procure these for me. He expected me to thaw a bit and become more communicative. I must have disappointed him for he soon left me.

This was the last time I was cross-examined.

The most exciting event during the rest of the day was a walk along the corridor outside to the washroom. I then saw a Canadian being taken into his cell. We looked at one another but did not get a chance to speak. For supper we got two pieces of bread. The rest of the day I read or slept, and at night I slept like a log right up to 6.30 a.m., when breakfast was served.

The meal was soon eaten – the two pieces of bread only made me want more. One of the tablets I had eaten in the boat probably contained more nourishment that the two pieces of bread. After breakfast I sat on the bed and read, waiting for further Germans to come into my cell to search for information.

It was eleven o'clock when the sub-lieutenant came in with the good news that I was to be taken to the English camp. I got up and with four Canadians was taken out of the hut and two hundred metres down a short road which ended at the gate of the prison camp. Not one word passed between us. The others evidently felt and thought the same as I did. It didn't bother me much being a prisoner. At that time I was very optimistic and thought I could manage to get home again in two months' time. What I thought would be so nice was to meet RAF officers once more, to talk to people who weren't German, to talk to friends.

I noticed that the Canadians' footsteps also went faster as we neared the place. Inside the gate a small group of prisoners waited eagerly for our arrival. 'Were there any old friends among the newcomers?' And our thoughts were, 'Is there anyone we know inside the fence?'

Only one of the Canadians and I saw no one we knew. The German who had brought us there and seen us safely through the gate disappeared and we were left to our allies. I did not know what to do so I kept a bit in the background and looked at the others. Soon we were surrounded by our fellow prisoners who deluged us with questions about everything under the sun – from baseball results to how we had got out alive. After a time, when their curiosity had been satisfied, the group gradually dispersed. They sauntered back to their huts in small groups.

A small red-haired squadron leader came up to me and introduced himself as the oldest prisoner in the camp. He was very friendly and told me among other things what would happen to us in the near future. This camp was only a temporary one. The place could hold eighty men, not counting the permanent staff. As soon as this number was reached, the required German guard was detailed, food distributed and prisoners sent by train to the so-called Stammlager. Durchgangslager Frankfurt needed about fourteen days to be quite full. Later, during the autumn of 1942, when the RAF started air raids on a large scale, it was necessary to enlarge the camp. Now only one-third of the places were occupied, and I could reckon on being in the camp for a week or ten days.

The squadron leader showed me around the place. We went first into one of the huts, to the room I was to sleep in. From there to the bathroom, the mess, the library (a cupboard in one corner of the mess), and at length to the canteen, where we could buy small things like ashtrays, picture frames, shaving articles, etc. I wondered where the money would come from and was told that the prisoners received part of their wages in German marks – not in ordinary marks which could be used in Germany but in special paper notes only valid in the camp. We could expect to get some of this money in a couple of days. As we walked along, the squadron leader had not asked any questions concerning military affairs, and I was glad because I was thus spared the unpleasantness of not answering them.

When we arrived back at the hut where I was to live he left me. Lunch hour in the camp was half past twelve and I had about half an hour left. I went into the living room. Five or six men in RAF uniforms were sitting there. I sat down on a stool and took a magazine. It would be good to have a look at one's fellow prisoners before chumming up with them. In England we had been told so much about this camp, hidden microphones, Germans in English uniforms and other gadgets that I thought it best to be cautious. My fellow prisoners were evidently of the same opinion because they talked together in a very reserved and cautious manner. They seemed on their guard.

Then lunch hour arrived and all prisoners – we were ten officers and about twenty sergeants – trooped into our respective messes. I had expected a very spartan meal, consisting mainly of tea substitute, and was greatly surprised to see the table laid with toast, butter, jam and cakes. The tea itself was excellent. In time I learned how this comparatively good standard of food was kept up. This was one of the first camps to be formed for RAF personnel and had therefore a good regular connection with the International Red Cross. Food was packed and sent from England to Switzerland and from there the

Red Cross sent it on to prisoner of war camps. The ration was one five-kilogram parcel per man per week, but on account of the through traffic this camp received more parcels than there were men and could thus accumulate a reserve fund of food. When there were new arrivals there was usually a sort of feast and this very much helped to raise their spirits.

After the meal I sat talking to the camp leader and adjutant in the dining room. The others left after a while and we were finally quite alone. Then the door opened and a tall man entered the room. I had seen him before somewhere.

'Didn't you once fly a Mosquito from Shetland in 1942?'* I blurted out. He looked at me coldly and with a dismissive remark ridiculed my question. Suddenly I remembered where I was and understood his behaviour.

Soon afterwards I went out to have a look at the camp and take in my surroundings. The piece of ground on

---

* The 331 Squadron was first based at Orkney, but was split in two in December 1941, and a detachment sent to Sumburgh in Shetland. Müller joined the latter on 4 February 1942. Guhnfeldt describes a Beaufort torpedo bomber mission to Norway in March where Beauforts were lost, but he does not mention a Mosquito mission. But there might have been other missions over Norway from Sumburgh. Most of the missions flown by 331 in Shetland were aimed at German reconnaissance missions flown out of Stavanger, but it seems that very few German planes were shot down at this stage of the war. Later, with the development of a more sophisticated radar system in the Northern Isles, tracking became easier.

which the camp was built could very well measure seventy by fifty metres, and three huts plus the mess made up the buildings. A small road went round the hut on the inside of the fence. As a rule our daily exercise consisted of walking round and round this road. I started – it took four minutes to make one round. I looked at the fence while I walked. It was about two and a half metres high; barbed wire was stretched between solid wooden posts. Two fences, one inside the other, with a one-metre space in between. In the area between them, barbed-wire 'loops' lay loose on the ground. The barbed-wire fences were not difficult to climb over, the danger lay in being caught in the loops. But the fence was not the only hindrance if one wished to get home again. I walked on along the edge of the road. A low wooden fence was put up about five metres inside the nearest fence. One of the first things the camp chief told me was that if I valued my life I would not go beyond this fence. German guards had orders to shoot without warning if a prisoner got outside the 'warning wire'. And there were enough guards about. One of them patrolled the road outside the gate and in the four corners of the camp guards were posted in towers with their eyes on the camp.

For the time being I saw no possibility of getting out and in annoyance I had turned my steps towards the library to get a book when the tall man from the dining room came towards me.

This time he smiled broadly and shook hands with me. The picture from Sumburgh again came to my mind.

It was a cold sunny day at the end of March 1942. The Norwegian fighter squadron was stationed on the Orkney Islands and had received orders to send a flight up to Sumburgh on the south point of the Shetlands because they had had several visits by German reconnaissance planes up there. Well, this sunny morning I and some others were on watch, and I can clearly remember the smart Mosquito which landed there. It was the first time I had seen a Mosquito and I tried to get into conversation with its pilot. He was not talkative – only said he was on his way to Norway where he would take photographs. He had just landed at Sumburgh to get his radio in order and fill up with fuel. While the mechanics worked we ordered food for him and his radio operator. They sat at a table in the dispersal room and ate in silence. As soon as the plane was ready they thanked us and were off.

We stood watching the plane climb eastwards and then disappear. That same evening the control officers told us that that very plane was missing – shot down by fighter planes. The airman, whom we all at that time thought was killed, was now beside me and recounted roughly what had happened. Everything had gone well on the trip over. They had taken a number of photos of Trondheim Fjord and the German naval base there.* On the way back they were attacked by Germans. The plane caught

---

* The Dora I submarine base in Trondheim. Construction was begun in autumn 1941, and it was handed over to the Kriegsmarine in the summer of 1943 and became the home base for the 13th U-boat Flotilla.

fire and they had to make an emergency landing in some field south of the fjord. German infantry was on the spot. The airman and wireless operator had only just time to help the fire in the plane a bit with the signal pistol when they were caught. They sat in prison in Trondheim for two days before being sent by rail to Akershus prison in Oslo. They were there for over a week before continuing on to Germany, to Dulag Luft, Frankfurt. He told us many small episodes from Akershus. About Norwegian girls working in the prison who helped prisoners. It was ages since I had spoken to anyone who had been in my hometown Oslo, and I asked how everything was there, but of course he could not tell me much because the journey from the railway station to Akershus had been by the police bus, called 'Black Mary'.

He was now a member of the permanent camp staff. His wireless operator was safe in Stammlager Luft III. It was fun talking to him and the time passed quickly as we tramped six or seven kilometres round and round inside the fence. Then we parted.

The library was still open and I found a book which looked interesting. With this as a companion I found a spot in the sunshine and remained there until the other camp dwellers began to saunter towards the mess hut. It was time for the evening meal.

The tea table that afternoon had rather impressed me, but the one they laid out now was beyond anything I could have expected as a prisoner. If this continued I would not mind being a prisoner of war. As a little welcoming treat for us newcomers a film was shown in the sergeants' mess after supper.

The show ended about one hour before the doors to the huts were closed by the Germans and everyone had to be in his respective hut. I had as yet not met my room mates. They were sitting there when I came in. Both were Canadians and their names were Bill and Hank. We sat on our beds and chatted a bit before turning in. The conversation was mostly about small topics but also touched on subjects about which we felt it best to be careful. We only spoke a little about what we did before the war, where we lived and what work we had. Bill, a tall, thin, pale chap, had worked in a bank in Winnipeg. He was also newly married. His wife was in Canada. He proudly showed us photos of her. Hank was from Calgary and studied engineering before the war but broke off his studies to join the air force. He was of medium height and quite handsome in spite of his face being burned in places. I guessed he had flown a Spitfire. It was mostly those fellows who got burned on the face. I had seen many such in England. The fuel tanks in the Spitfires were in front of the cockpit and if they caught fire it was almost impossible to get out of the machine without getting burned. Later my guess was confirmed. Hank had flown with a squadron belonging to our wing, but which was stationed at another airfield.

All three of us were tired after the day's events and went to bed early. I fell asleep as soon as my head touched the pillow.

A ferret at the exit of one of the discovered tunnels.

A replica goon tower at Stalag Luft III.

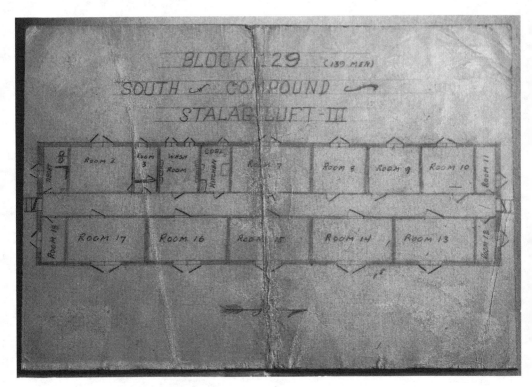

A typical barracks hut layout as drawn by an American POW.

A recreated barracks hut at the POW Camps Museum, Żagań.

Per Bergsland (left) with Jens Müller at Muskoka, Ontario in 1944 © Cato Guhnfeldt Collection.

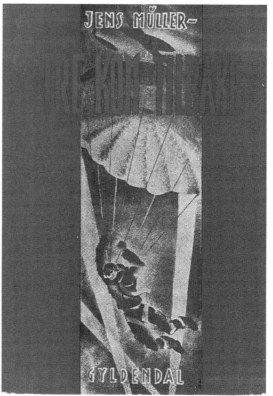

The book jacket of the Norwegian edition of Müller's memoir, first published in 1946.

The unassuming boulder and inscription are the Müller family's acknowledgement of Jen's modesty. The memorial is at Bryn Church, Rykkinn, close to the home of Jen's son Jon © Jon Müller.

Memorial to 'The 50' prisoners from Stalag Luft III in Poland who were murdered by the Nazis after being recaptured.

I was in the camp about ten days before we were moved on. We got notice the day before. Bedclothes, except blankets, were handed in. Early next morning we had breakfast for the last time in Dulag Luft I. They distributed one day's bread ration to each man. One after the other our names were called and we were let out of the gate, one by one. It took time to get us all out as the identity of each prisoner had to be checked with the help of photographs or cards.

Well, we got out at last. We marched towards the town in double file. Our escort consisted of two armed guards. Many of us thought of escape. We soon changed our minds when we saw one prisoner who was slightly out of line pushed back with the muzzle of a gun, followed by warnings in harsh German. The chances of being free for long were very small, even if one managed to run beyond the range of the gun. It took about twenty minutes to get to the railway station. It was not in Frankfurt itself but in one of the suburbs. We had expected an extra train or at least a couple of carriages to be standing ready and to be hurried on to them as soon as we got there. But we waited on the platform of one of the side lines for over an hour and a half before the carriage arrived and we got in. Another hour went by before the train to which our carriage would be added arrived. The carriage was furnished like our third-class compartment carriages. Eight men in each compartment. We were given some Red Cross parcels for the journey. Two men were responsible for the fair distribution of the provisions.

Thus began the journey to the camp which was to be my abode for almost two years.

Even before the train had started, the bench felt very hard and there was very little room. But these were no cattle trucks so we had no complaints to make. Hour after hour the train rattled along. Now and again it stopped for half an hour; once it waited for two hours. I expected one or another of us would try to cut his journey short by disappearing into the landscape, but most of us saw how hopeless it would be to get away in our British uniform and without help of any sort. So the journey continued uneventfully for the whole day. Food was distributed at regular intervals. I tried to make out the direction we were taking but all I gathered was that we were generally going eastwards. The names of the stations were quite unknown. I gave up in the end.

The day passed and night too, slowly. There was not much sleep to be had. The next day was just like the first. The train worked its way slowly east with long pauses. At last, late in the evening on the second day, we heard the guard say we had arrived. It was dark. In the dim light of the blue lamps we could see that the train had stopped in a siding of a large station. Bright lights shone against the sky towards the south and we guessed it was from the camp we were going to. The lights from the watchtowers swept the horizon now and then. It could not be many hundred metres away. We expected to be marched off at once but got orders to remain in the carriage until the next morning. It was cold that night and we slept badly. Men from the camp redoubled the guard and the carriage was floodlit on the outside. The Germans were taking no chances. Morning came at last, and at six o'clock we headed to the camp, which we reached in ten minutes. In the daylight we had our guesses confirmed regarding the size of the station. It was evidently a very large railway junction. I asked the guard what its name was and in what part of Germany. But he had received his instructions and only smiled and shrugged his shoulders. When we left the train only a fence with a gate separated us from the road. We followed the road straight eastwards for a couple of hundred metres, turned to the right and followed a new road a couple of hundred metres more before we came to the road which led westwards to the camp. It was only a walk of five or six hundred metres. On this last bit of road to our right was a German labour camp. A group was exercising with spades as we passed by. This amused us a great deal, especially the Canadians. A little further away was the front camp or 'Vorlager' as the Germans called it, with hospital, gaol and store buildings. We passed the whole of the front camp and some of the German labour camp before reaching the gate leading into our 'rest home'.

I went through the door with an odd mixture of excitement and curiosity, past the guard and the German flag, turned to the left and stood still with the other prisoners in front of the gate in the barbed-wire fence. They counted us before letting us pass through. The Germans took us right into an empty hut where we were told to wait. We waited an hour before being called, one by one, in alphabetical order, for body searching. This went slowly and systematically. My turn did not come before ten o'clock. A German stood behind a table in blue overalls; he told me to empty my pockets and undress. I did so. The sign 'Norway' on my uniform jacket interested him and he started talking of Norway. He had been stationed there for some months before coming to this camp and had evidently liked it. He didn't examine me very thoroughly, and while he talked I dressed and put all my things in my pockets. Feeling relieved, I went out to the others who were ready and sat and waited in the sunshine outside. I had rescued my fountain pen. I was told that fountain pens were not allowed in the camp. The German had been so interested in talking about Norway that he forgot to take it away from me. By eleven or half past all the examinations were over and we walked the last part of the road to the gate leading into the prison camp itself. The same thing took place here as in Dulag, only on a larger scale. Instead of a small flock of old prisoners receiving the new ones there were over one hundred who stood waiting anxiously inside the gate.

Again I looked about for any familiar faces, and to my joy saw one. He too recognized me and came towards me with a smile. It gave me great pleasure to see him again. His name was Don, a Canadian from Toronto, and I was not only glad at meeting an old acquaintance so far away in Germany, but also at unexpectedly finding him still alive.

We had trained together in England in the Operational Training Unit, which was the last part of our training before being sent to an active squadron.* He was the best of our bunch. As soon as he was ready he was sent to North Africa, to a Hurricane squadron. A long time afterwards I had heard he had been shot down and killed soon after his arrival. Well, here he was in Stalag Luft III! It was a great treat to see him. But we had not said much to one another before an authoritative English voice asked all newcomers to go to the canteen building, where lunch was being served. At the mention of food I found that the food packet on the train had not been very satisfying. Don showed me the way to the canteen and left me to myself until I had appeased my hunger.

The canteen was soon thronging with old and new prisoners. There was more talk than eating of the dried salted fish and potatoes. This was understandable as even the old prisoners turned up their noses at the fish – it was unappetizing. But the potatoes were not bad. I stood alone nibbling a potato and watching the confusion. I noticed a pair of bright, brown eyes fixed on me. The face was an agreeable one. Black hair, curly, short. He looked brown and healthy. He pushed his way through the crowd of prisoners and came up to me. 'Have you anywhere to live?' he asked and his English told me he was a New Zealander.

---

* This was probably at RAF Catterick, Yorkshire, where the members of 331 Squadron arrived in July 1941.

'No,' I said.

'We have an empty place, if you haven't anything better. My name is Ivan and I'm called Pop.'

Gratefully I accepted his invitation and introduced myself. Pop seemed full of life and energy. He immediately started to get me a cup, a knife and fork. Then he took me along to the hut he lived in and into the room. Most of its other inhabitants were there and sat about the room on beds or at the table.

Pop introduced 'Wally', tall and thin, sinewy, with a thin pale face. 'Birky', large and strong, broad face, curly brown hair. 'Scruff', small, agile and supple, with his face badly burned. 'Sparges', a man of the world, black hair; he stared intently into the eyes of the person he spoke to. Sam, a quiet little fellow, serious, red-haired and freckled. All of them Canadians. John, the only Englishman, was small and young, with fair, curly hair. A narrow unusual face. 'Pop' himself was the oldest and a New Zealander. They were all open and friendly.

The room was cosy and tidy. Four double bunks along the walls. Four double wardrobes in different parts of the room. A large table in the middle of the floor, two long benches and two small stools. From old packing cases and bits of planks, bookcases and a kitchen bench had been made. A stove in one corner. A large number of photographs and cuttings above each bed. It all looked comfortable and inviting compared to the rooms in Dulag. I had hardly time to take in this rough picture of the room and its inhabitants before they took the things

I was holding – food and toilet articles – and placed me on one of the stools at the table. Bread and a cup of tea were put before me. The talk started. At first I only answered questions about news from England. I was still careful of what I said, but understood they could all be trusted. The conversation soon grew lively. They gave an account of daily life in the camp, what the prisoners did and what the Germans did. All seven of them had been prisoners for about a year. They had only been in Stammlager Luft III for two months. The camp was quite new. Before that they had all been in a place on the Baltic called Barth. This was a better camp, except for the food, which was bad. Red Cross parcels had not yet arrived. German rations were no good. Our staple food consisted of potatoes and these were scarce now. But they hoped things would improve very soon. I liked these seven fellows better and better. As we sat there a head appeared at the door saying that all newcomers were to meet in the canteen at four o'clock. The chief had something to tell them.

It was evidently tea time and the table was laid and Sam came back with a pile of slices of bread. Pop fetched a teapot and a jug of hot water. We had been sitting around the table talking for a long while when someone came in and asked if there were a Norwegian in the room.

'Yes,' I said.

'You'd better hurry up,' he said. 'The whole crowd are waiting in the canteen.'

I looked anxiously at the clock. Ten past four. I rushed out, and sure enough the canteen was full of people, all new arrivals, plus the senior officer. As I excused myself for coming so late he only asked me to be more punctual in future. Then I found a place among the others.

They welcomed us to the camp, to the RAF station. Even though we were now prisoners it didn't mean we could lie down and sleep all day. No, there was much work to be done. We would be told and shown in time what sort of work it would be. Meantime we could take it easy for a fortnight or so until we were more used to the new life. Later on we would be put to the work which best suited each one of us. Next morning we would attend a conference with one of the old prisoners. With a 'Good luck', the senior officer ended his speech and left us.

Wrapped in our own thoughts, we sauntered out of the canteen, each one to his own room. The rest of the evening was spent fetching bedclothes and getting fixed up as best as possible. My belongings were only the clothes I had on plus a razor from Dulag. But in a very short time my room mates gave me all the clothes and toilet articles I needed. They had received clothes from home and each one found something he could do without. Enriched with my new belongings and with a couple of potatoes in my stomach I went to bed and slept like a log.

Thus my life as a prisoner began in earnest. As the days went by I got more and more used to the daily life in the camp. I was lucky with my room mates. We got along fine. They were genuine, good-hearted fellows who helped me all they could. I made good use of the library, which was much larger and better equipped than the one at Dulag. An interesting subject soon cropped up, giving me food for study. Then I found other subjects and had to plan out my day's work in order to use my time well. And it flew. I wrote home and to my friends in Canada asking for food, clothes and books.

'You can expect results in four or five months,' my room mates told me. Like all new prisoners, I was sure of getting back to England again before five months had passed.

The fourteen days allowed for new prisoners to take it easy were soon gone. The British intelligence officer had cross-examined me with the others and found everything in order. After more than one hundred circuits walking inside the fence I knew the camp premises pretty well. I also became acquainted with several of my fellow prisoners but had as yet not noticed any underground work. Wally, Birky and Scruffy were absent from the room for several hours at a time. They were not in the library, they didn't make rounds, and took no part in any of the classes. But they returned to the room looking pale and tired and as a rule went straight to bed. There was certainly something going on behind the scenes.

I was too new in the camp to be included in any schemes. I kept myself occupied. Read a great deal, walked circuits and took part in gymnastics arranged by an Englishman. The food gradually improved. Red Cross parcels began to arrive so we were not starving. And we could go in for sport and gymnastics. When the weather was so bad that it wasn't fun to walk circuits, or when I was tired of reading, I started making things: teaspoons, bookcases and kitchen utensils. The spoons and small gadgets I made came in handy.

The fact that I could use my hands a bit helped me, without my realizing it, to a small job in the underground organization. One evening Wally came home after one of his customary absences and asked quite casually if I could make a large pair of bellows. I was sure this could be done if we could find the right materials and tools. Tools were strictly prohibited in the camp, and all sorts of materials, from nails to pieces of wood and string were very hard to get. Wally grew very thoughtful but said no more.

A couple of days later he asked me to join him after the roll call when the Germans had left. He took me to a room in one of the huts. Several other men were there. Some were changing into old shabby clothes. We waited there for some minutes. Wally was soon having an earnest conversation with one of these men. I just stood by, looking at them. A certain atmosphere of excitement was in the air. The climax came when a man stuck his head in at the door and said: 'All clear.'

At that moment it was obvious that everyone worked according to a plan. Everyone, with the exception of four men, went over to one side of the room. The other four swung aside one of the double bedsteads, removed a cover, and began to scrape away dust from one of the cracks in the floor. They soon found what they were looking for. Two small loops were fished out of the cracks. A couple of men pulled at these loops with two hooks, and a large piece of the floor was lifted out. The floor was double layered. The one underneath consisted of short wooden planks placed between the beams which supported the floor. Four or five of these planks were taken out. The ground under the building then became visible. All the huts were built on short posts driven into the sand, which stuck up thirty or forty centimetres above the surface. If one stood outside and bent over one could look under the whole building, except in a couple of places where the space in between was covered with planks. The slope which we could see through the hole in the floor was therefore well lit up by daylight from the sides. A couple of fellows in old clothes, and knotted handkerchiefs on their heads started digging in the sand directly under the hole. The upper coating of dry, rather grey sand was first carefully removed and put into a small box that was beside them, ready for such use. Then sand further down was removed and put into a bag. The two men worked while the sweat poured off them. Time was short. At last a spade hit wood. The last handful of sand was taken up.

The hole was square now, about half a metre each way and just as deep. One of the men who were digging bent down in the hole and pulled at two loops fastened to a wooden frame which was now visible. With an effort this was loosened and lifted up into the room. A large hole gaped at us down there. He jumped down, crept into a tunnel and disappeared. A dim yellowish light soon lit up the place down there. I heard him rummaging.

Some loose planks and packing sacks appeared and were thrown up. Finally a strange apparatus came into view. This was also pushed up. Now Wally became active. He took hold of the apparatus, asked me to go with him and left the room. I followed him somewhat unwillingly. It was the first time I had seen a tunnel of this sort and I would have liked to stay on for a while.

Wally went into the adjoining room. The fellows there were sitting at the supper table. They did not turn a hair at the sight of Wally, the apparatus and me. They simply made room on the floor. One could easily make out what sort of apparatus it was when it was on the floor. An air pump or bellows, roughly made of wood slats and a canvas kit-bag. One man sat at one end of the pump and worked the bellows in and out. A pair of valves in the end plate let the air in and out as it was meant to. Primitive but no doubt effective when in working order.

At present it was in a half-rotten and dilapidated condition, having been steadily in use for several months in the damp tunnel. The leather valves were not working and did not close as they should. The bellows were rotten and full of holes. The framework was worn out and shaky. Wally stood for a time thinking and looking at the pump, then turned to me and said it had to be in working condition by tomorrow evening. Could I manage it if I had a man to help me? Having hoped and waited ever since I arrived in the camp for some job like this I was of course happy at being given such a chance, especially as I was sure I could manage it. Wally and I figured out how much material was needed, and he then went to talk to the prisoner who was in charge of 'stores'.

I began to have an idea that the underground work, of which I hitherto knew nothing, was being carried out on a large scale.

I carried the pump back to the entrance of the tunnel and saw that the hole was closed for the night. It took about four minutes to get the frame in place, the sand in the hole thrown in, and tramped hard, all traces of the work carefully removed and the trapdoor closed. Cracks were filled with sand and the bed and patched rug put into place. All traces of the entrance were gone.

The pump was repaired next day and installed in the tunnel. This was my first work as a prisoner. The following week I made a new pump and installed it in the tunnel. With a knotted handkerchief on my head and dressed in an old pair of woollen combies I crept down through the hole which I had until then only seen from above. The tunnel went directly eastwards towards the pine grove just outside the camp. Behind me it was extended westwards up to the neighbouring hut. There was also another entrance and this was used to take the sand up and out of the tunnel.

I had in my hand a small lamp made out of a tin box filled with melted margarine, and with pieces of the pump and some tools I crawled in. The tunnel was quite narrow. It was impossible to crawl in it on one's knees. One had to creep along on one's stomach. It wasn't too difficult if I grabbed hold of the frames of the wooden shoring and hauled myself along. The air down there was damp and stale. I soon tired from the unusual exercise. I was clumsy and often scraped my back against the frame-members in the ceiling, although I kept as flat as I could on my belly. It was odd being shut up in this tight, dark, damp hole only dimly lit by a small oil lamp. Perspiring, I finally reached the first bend in the tunnel. The passage had fallen in here and the tunnel was dug around the loose part. With some effort I managed to get everything I had with me around the corner to the right and could continue to crawl further. Now the tunnel made a small turn to the left so as to continue in its intended direction. At the same time it sloped downwards deeper under the surface. It was hard to understand how the fellows who dug could keep track of the direction, since they had no measuring instruments. The next bend in the tunnel was at the deepest point. Here a vertical shaft went up a couple of metres. Then it continued forwards again a short distance where a new vertical shaft came to view. It went straight up about three metres and was lined with wooden panels. A room for tools and materials was dug out at the top, which was also used as a pump room.

I was now directly underneath the south end of the canteen building. The concrete floor was the only thing separating me from the room above. I could hear the orchestra practising over my head. Every time there was digging in the tunnel the orchestra practised. This drowned the noise of the working pump.

I installed the pump and crawled back to the room with the trapdoor.

I returned to my own room full of admiration for the men who had worked and dug the hole, and happy to at last have a small part in the work to get out and home. Over the next two weeks, however, there was no more work for me, and I went back to my books. But I felt restless and could not concentrate. This was partly because I hoped to take part when the tunnel was ready and partly on account of the weather. They were lovely sunny weeks. Most of the prisoners lay outside the huts and sunned themselves and grew browner and browner.

One such sunny morning, while I lay in the sand gazing at a book, the camp's fire truck drove up at a good speed. It contained ten or twelve Germans in overalls. Something was up. Hoses were laid out from a water tank in the camp and up to one of the huts nearest the gate. Meanwhile the hut's inhabitants were chased out and guards placed outside. I had seen a couple of hut searches during my time there and they took place in the same manner. The only new thing this time was the fire truck and hose that they laid out. There was no smoke or fire to be seen. I waited anxiously for what was going to happen. The hose was put under the northern part of the hut. Two or three Germans crawled underneath the hut and disappeared for a time, then they crawled out again to fetch the nozzle of the hose. I asked a friend what was going on and was informed that the tunnel under the hut had been discovered and the Germans were now using water to collapse it. So there was another tunnel. I had thought the one I had seen was the camp's only one. This set my imagination working. There could very possibly be two tunnels under each hut, for all I knew. Best to ask Wally.

He stood apart watching the Germans' activities with disapproval. I felt I could ask what was up now I had seen one of the tunnels. Wally answered most of my questions. At present there were two tunnels being dug, the one I had seen and another one, plus the one now discovered. There were different parties working on each respective tunnel. The parties worked as units quite independent of each other. A man with initiative and some experience of digging worked out a plan and asked fifteen or twenty men if they would join him and have a go. When the necessary number of men was reached the leader went to the senior officer to get the plan approved. All the plans were more or less alike: 'We have in mind to dig a tunnel from here and out of the camp and either walk or go by train home to England.' These tunnel schemes were usually approved.

It was different with schemes to make a hole in the fence or to jump over it in the dark, or to dress up as a German and walk past the guard with the help of false papers. These schemes had to be well thought out in order to be approved. There were very few who tried them. The fence was considered too dangerous and the bluff method needed very good clothes and papers to have the slightest chance of succeeding. The majority preferred the tunnels. It took time but the risk was small, and if successful one could as a rule get well on one's way before the break was discovered.

Now when I look back and think of the tunnels dug in this first camp and compare them to the one we completed a year later in the new camp, I understand how inefficient the work was and what a poor chance there was of success. In the first camp the different kinds of work were not specialized. If one wanted to escape one had to take care of everything: make clothes and false papers, get food and other equipment, besides digging and carrying sand. In other words, one had to be an all-round handyman. Later on, things were arranged more rationally. Different departments were formed where individual experience and talents were made better use of. But a one hundred per cent specialization did not take place unitl the new part of the camp was in use.

The small groups continued to dig, make clothes and papers, collect money and equipment. Inefficient watch systems among the prisoners enabled the Germans to discover the tunnels. Of all the attempts made, only one succeeded during the eight months I was there. That was the celebrated case of the 'Wooden Horse'. But work continued with the same degree of optimism. Sooner or later we would succeed in digging a tunnel leading from our huts to the woods outside.

I worked for three weeks in a small tunnel, hauling out sand and pumping fresh air in to those who were digging.

This tunnel was discovered one morning during the roll call, and I was out of work for some time.

Some days later a new batch of prisoners were brought in, and among them was a Norwegian. His name was Haldor, from Bergen.* One of the most charming chaps I ever met. We walked rounds together and forgot time and place while we talked of mutual friends in Norway and of the future. He belonged to my squadron, 331 Norwegian, but had joined it after I was shot down. He had news from England.

Unfortunately Haldor didn't remain long in the camp. The Germans had a camp in Poland, Szubin, which would be partly occupied by prisoners from Stalag Luft III, until a new section of our camp was being built. Haldor was among those who had to leave.

Per, or 'Pete' as he was called, was the next Norwegian to arrive, but he was also to be sent to Szubin.† Like many other Norwegian airmen, 'Pete' had flown under a false name, an English one, for precautionary reasons. They were men who were on the German black list

---

* Haldor Espelid. He was shot down by flak over France on 27 August 1942. He was held prisoner for a while at Lager 31B at Szubin near Lvov, before he went to Stalag Luft III, where he participated in the great escape. He was captured and shot, and buried in an unknown grave. His younger sister Ingrid became the face of Norwegian home cooking for decades with her television cookery shows.

† Per Bergsland, the other Norweigan who made it through the great escape. He was shot down on the French side of the Channel on 19 August 1942 during the Dieppe raid.

before escaping from Norway and were not certain the Germans would respect the Geneva Convention if they were taken prisoner.

The day we all said goodbye to those who were to be sent to Poland was a memorable one. Don, the Canadian whom I had recognized on the day of my arrival, was among them. Each one of them hoped to be back again some time in spring when the new camp was ready.

Then I was once more the only Norwegian in the camp. A new lot of prisoners arrived but no Norwegians. The others told us, however, that there had been a Norwegian among them. He had tried to escape during the train journey and was shot in the attempt. The Germans took him off at one of the stations. His name was Jan, they said.* He was a big fellow who wore handcuffs and had a special guard. I guessed who it was. I had met him and knew his brother in Norway. The last people who saw him as he was being carried off the train were sure he was dead or dying.

Nevertheless, Jan turned up in the camp two months later. Somewhat thin and pale and slightly sunken-in on one side where the shot had gone through him, but happy and content. That he had survived a shot through

---

* Jan Staubo, shot down on the same mission as Bergsland. He attempted numerous escapes but remained a prisoner of war until the war ended. Although he took part in the planning of the great escape he was moved to another camp before the breakout. Later in life he became a member of the International Olympic Committee.

his right lung, a shot fired at a distance of a couple of yards, increased his self-confidence considerably and added to his joy of life.

My English room mate John had been sent to Poland, and Jan now took his place. It was astonishing how soon he recovered after the tough time he had been through and he soon became initiated into the routine of the camp.

Meantime the work on the new camp, which was to relieve the strain on ours, had progressed so far that the time had arrived to make a recreation ground. The Germans would not do this work so we sent a working party of twenty-four men over every day when the weather was fine. They had to promise not to try to escape on the way but come straight back after the day's work. Here we got an agreeable change in our prison routine and Jan and I joined up.

One fine morning after the roll call at ten we walked over to our work place. It was only a few hundred metres' walk, out of the main gate and past the German labour camp. The new camp seemed a paradise compared to the barren place we came from. The trees on the lot were still closely grouped around the huts and gave them a picturesque appearance. Spades, picks and axes were handed out. Work progressed the whole day until four o'clock. We cut trees and cleared the ground. The physical exercise felt good. We were hot and tired by the time we left for home again, and were enriched with nails, small bits of planks, dry wood and pieces of coal which we found inside and outside the huts and on the road. Next time I returned I would take time to look for more nails. These were much in demand and strictly prohibited in the camp.

We made many trips over to the new camp during the autumn, before the cold and the snow came in earnest. Besides the work on the playing field, the foundations were laid for a theatre.

The autumn passed quickly. Letters and parcels from home and from Canada and England gradually began to arrive. We also received some clothes from England. Many of the books and writing materials I had asked for started to arrive. We felt more and more comfortable. For a long time Jan and I were the only Norwegians in the camp, but newcomers told us that another Norwegian was on his way here.

Later in the autumn Kjell arrived.* He had lost his left hand when he was shot down and had been in hospital for some time. He now moved into our room. By the time winter arrived it was becoming overcrowded in the camp. There were too many men in most of the rooms. There were rumours that we would move into the new camp within a few weeks. But the weeks went by and

---

* Hans Kjell Hansen, who was later released in a prisoner exchange in October 1943 facilitated by the Red Cross. Hansen had lost a hand after he was shot down on 31 July 1942 and rescued by a German ship. He was the first Norwegian pilot to return from a PoW camp. See Guhnfeldt, *Spitfire Saga, Vol. II*, p. 158.

no move took place. Snow started falling. We started thinking of Christmas. We saved up biscuits, sugar, raisins and chocolate to be used in cakes. Sam was in charge of cakes and a master of the art. His cakes were mostly made of crushed biscuits and dried milk. My own time was taken up with a navigation course set up in the camp. Jan studied French.

Work on the tunnel went slowly now the snow was there. It was difficult not to leave traces when carrying sand away from the tunnel for dispersal under other huts. Besides, one could smell the damp sand from the tunnel a long way off. This odour was one of the strongest clues the Germans had to warn them that it was time to evacuate a hut and make a search. Therefore digging had almost ceased. We made plans for a spring campaign instead. When the weather improved, the tunnel would be completed in a fortnight. This could be managed by employing a sufficient number of men. Meantime it was only half finished and it had taken the small group of prisoners many months to get to the present stage. When the right time arrived, sometime in early spring, our committee would see to it that enough men were put on the job, then the remaining part of the tunnel could be finished within two weeks. Meanwhile all work was stopped and the camp had a breathing space. The Germans were relieved at this. The search parties and guards gradually grew more lenient. Christmas was approaching rapidly. Sam's cake-making and Wally's cooking made this day into a real feast. We and our guests consumed all the foodstuffs we had stored up. On Christmas Day everybody went around paying calls on each other. There was open house everywhere, and that Christmas was an experience I would not have missed for anything. Christmas festivities and the cakes lasted about a week. New Year's Eve was a fitting climax to it all.

The winter there in Germany was on the whole mild with very little snow. We soon noticed the first whiff of spring in the air and our plans for flight began to come to life again. Wally was now one of the leaders of the tunnel work and became very busy. Preparations for the last part of the digging were well on their way when he came home one day looking depressed. A stretch of tunnel had caved in and anyone walking there could fall through the frozen crust. The Germans had their usual patrols out and would surely discover the whole thing if something was not done at once to repair the damaged tunnel. The entire work force got busy but it was too late. Next day a German garbage cart sank through. The tunnel was found, and the only thing left was to try to save the pumps and tools before the huts were examined.

It was the last tunnel which was dug before we moved. In April we packed our belongings and moved over to the new camp. Some of us were to remain in the old place, but the majority were to move. Those who had been sent to Poland in the autumn were coming back to the old camp.

The move was a good excuse for the Germans to search all our belongings and they gave our persons and belongings a thorough going over. Everything prohibited was confiscated: fountain pens, cigarette lighters, large pocket knives and all sorts of carpentry tools. But they did not profit much by this search and were disappointed. They found little as we had mostly hidden away or camouflaged forbidden articles, and a packet or two of cigarettes went a long way towards making a German cooperative.

The search, getting our belongings onto the lorry again and ourselves dressed took an hour. We walked through the gate in one large troop and on towards our new camp.

Those who had lived together in the same hut in the old camp were allowed to choose adjoining rooms in one of the new huts. Each room was intended for six men. When the prisoners from Poland returned, we were promised that Haldor and Pete would move in with us. In the meantime we started turning one of the rooms into a combined dining and living room, and the other into a bedroom. This kept us busy for a couple of weeks. Chairs and bookcases had to be made from bits of wood found lying about the camp. Finally we managed to arrange quite a decent-looking living room. The bedrooms, however, were not attractive, since they were just full of bunks.

The best thing about moving was of course having something new to occupy our thoughts and to do. It took us out of our old routine and was fun while it lasted.

The first two months in the new camp were lively, not only because we were occupied getting our rooms and personal belongings in order, but also because attempts at escape were almost a daily occurrence. The strangest methods were tried just at that time when the Germans were occupied organizing things in the new camp. They thought we were too busy getting our things in order to think of anything else.

They were mistaken.

The Escape Committee started work just a couple of weeks after our arrival. Not as they had in the old camp, because now everything was to come under one leader. Each person's ability would be more effectively utilized. One man heading a committee of specialists from the various departments would direct and control everything which was to be done in connection with escape work. The chief was a lawyer by profession, and at the time I came to the camp he had been a prisoner for a couple of years, out of which six months had been spent as a 'guest' of the Gestapo for attempting to escape. He was the obvious leader where both experience and personality were concerned.

During our last winter in the old camp he had, assisted by a handful of the keenest and most experienced prisoners, planned the organization of the new camp. And he carried out the plan. All those taking part in escape work were assigned a department in which to work depending on the ability and experience of each man. The departments included: tunnel diggers, sand carriers, watchmen, carpenters, tailors, jacks of all trade, those who made identity papers, news, concentrated foodstuffs, maps, etc., etc.

The leaders of these departments were the chief's advisers.

The next problem was to provide contact between the chief and the prisoners. One man from each hut was chosen as the chief's spokesman. Messages and orders from the chief, or 'Big X' as he was called, were given to the prisoners through the 'small Xs'.

As in the old camp, now called the East Compound, two or three Germans sauntered about the new camp, from the time the hut doors were opened early in the morning until they were closed after dark in the evening. At night a guard patrolled with a dog. These fellows had the sole task of ferreting out anything that was 'Verboten'.

If we were ever to get any real work done we had to have our own watchmen and signalling system. We had to know how many Germans were in the camp, where they were and what they were doing from one minute to the next. Watchmen and an intelligence department were therefore the first to be established. The system worked very well when the digging commenced.

The main work started with the digging of three tunnels. All the experience gained from similar work in the old camp was put into it. The trapdoors leading down into the tunnels, which up to now had been the weak point which usually led to discovery of the tunnels, were extremely carefully constructed. As it happened, the Germans themselves had been considerate enough to help us a long way with this. Unlike the arrangement in the old huts, a foundation had been laid under each room in the new huts. This consisted of a large square block which was meant to carry the weight of the stove and chimney. It was not difficult to see that the most convenient place for a tunnel entrance was through just such a foundation.

Three Poles were masters at making the new entrances. These tunnels were christened 'Tom', 'Dick' and 'Harry'.

'Tom', in the most south-westerly hut, was the least safe of the three; the one most open to discovery. It was also the only one which was discovered. Here the Poles had chiselled a hole in the cement floor at the base of the brick chimney in the room adjoining the washroom. They stole cement and cast a block which fitted exactly into the hole. The inevitable cracks between the 'lid' and the hole were filled with soft clay and sprinkled with dust and dry cement each time the cover was put on. When a couple of garbage tins were put on top the chances of discovery were small.

The entrance to 'Dick' was the most ingenious of the three, in the drainage tank in the washroom floor in the neighbouring hut to 'Tom'. The Poles had done good work with this entrance. When the wooden grating was in place over the square mouth of the shallow well it was practically impossible to discover anything wrong with the concrete. In addition, the well was always half full of water because the water outlet was located halfway up one sidewall. The hole was so narrow that a broad-shouldered man could not get out of it without help, he had to be hauled out. The trapdoor was ingenious: one sidewall had been chiselled away, and the shaft to the tunnel sunk behind the wall. A concrete plate could be slid into the place of the removed sidewall. When soft clay had been moulded into the cracks and corners and the well filled with water it took a very close examination by a practised eye to discover the fake.

To open the trapdoor the well had to be emptied, the soft clay removed and the plate lifted out. With practice the job of closing the trap could be done in seconds.

The entrance to 'Harry' was made in hut 104, in a room on the west side and at the northern end of the building. In this hut each room had a small cast-iron stove. The stove weighed fifty kilos and two men could lift it quite easily. It stood in the corner nearest the door. The floor in this corner was covered with tiles as protection against falling embers. The tile-covered area measured some one and a half metres each side and rested on the brick foundation under the hut. The Poles lifted out the tiles first. They then removed sufficient bricks from the middle of the foundation so that one man could get down into the hole quite comfortably, continuing until sand was reached. The floor tiles were then fastened with cement to a wooden board the same size as the area covered by the tiles. Hinges were procured somehow or other and fastened to the trapdoor and a floor beam. The frame with tiles could now be swung into place over the hole, and when the dust from the floor was swept down into the fine cracks and the stove put in place, the entrance had completely disappeared.

The Escape Committee had been extremely active while these entrances were being built. A list of available material was made out. Information about the German alarm system was obtained through the friendly cooperation of a couple of German guards. These 'tame Goons' were a great help to us even though they were unaware of it. They helped us to obtain tools which we could not make ourselves – such as hammers, pliers, files, metal saws, etc. Ever since the camp was started and the tame Goons discovered, they had, in the presence of witnesses, accepted so much Red Cross food and so many cigarettes that they were in the uncomfortable situation of being obliged to obey orders given to them by prisoners. I got an idea of how well they obeyed orders when the department chiefs were asked at a meeting what tools they needed. The list was quite a long one. Nevertheless a couple of days later all these items were delivered to the camp.

These same Germans told us that sound detectors were placed underground all along the fence at regular intervals. These detectors resembled seismographs and would pick up sounds within a distance of five to ten metres and register on an alarm system in the guardhouse. However, it was impossible to find out exactly where these detectors were placed. It was therefore decided to dig the tunnels so deep that they were out of range of these seismographs. Eight metres under the surface should be sufficiently deep, according to information received from the Germans. And the shafts for 'Tom', 'Dick' and

'Harry' were dug accordingly. A very busy period started for me too. The department to which I belonged was to be responsible for making three air pumps, and trolleys to carry sand from the tunnel face back to the shaft.

All the Norwegians were employed in different departments. Some of them dug, some sewed, others did carpentry or were on duty as watchmen. The whole camp was gradually drawn into the work.

The German watch was comparatively slack in the first month. There were hours during the day when there were no Germans at all in the camp. We took full advantage of this, and also of the fact that groups of trees were still in the camp and shut us off to some extent from the view of the guard towers.

We got rid of large quantities of sand from the shafts and tunnels by simply spreading it over the paths which led between the huts. These roads were covered with the same kind of sand which we dug out of the tunnels. As long as it was fresh it had the same light-yellow colour too. As the days passed the sand on the roads became greyer from all the dust round about and the tunnel sand gradually became conspicuous. It did not take long for the Germans to notice the new sand which daily appeared on the roads. A search was made but nothing found. However, many more patrols were put on watch in the camp. This did not prevent our spreading sand on the roads. It was done as follows: bags were made of canvas from kitbags, bags narrow enough to be put inside the trouser legs of the carriers. They hung on a loop which was placed around the man's neck. These bags had an opening at either end. The lower end could be pinned shut with a pin made of steel wire stuck in and out through holes made on the lower edge of the canvass. String was fastened to each pin and ran up to the trouser pocket of the carrier. The bags were filled by means of large funnels. Then the carriers walked about the camp in pairs in lively conversation. At a suitable moment they put their hands in their trouser pockets, pulled at the string, the pins pulled out, the bottom of the bag opened and out ran the sand onto the road.

Thus for a long time we managed to get rid of the sand without mishap, thanks to good cooperation between our watchmen, the tunnel diggers, and sand carriers. The work progressed slowly but surely. As the work went more and more smoothly the leaders had a number of other things to do. Prisoners turned up daily with various practical or fantastic plans for escape, from sneaking out as stowaways in the camp's garbage lorry, to floating over the fence by means of a hot-air balloon. Fortunately not many of these plans were approved.

The few which were approved usually required a good deal of preliminary work in the form of clothes, papers and other equipment. One attempt which succeeded, and whereby twenty-five men got out of the camp, was a very economical affair as far as equipment was concerned. The twenty-five men walked out of the main gate in broad daylight, right past the guard, who opened the gates wide for them. Strangely enough, what started the whole thing was lice in one of the huts. The prisoners complained and the Germans took immediate measures to remedy this state of affairs in the bathhouse situated in the 'Vorlager' of the old camp.

Twenty-four prisoners were lined up inside the gate for inspection by an armed German guard. The guard's papers were checked, and the twenty-four men were marched to delousing. About an hour later they returned and a new lot were sent out. This procedure was repeated until the required number of prisoners were deloused.

A Dutchman happened to be among the prisoners. He spoke German like a native and was chosen to impersonate the German guard. A German uniform which the tailoring department had in stock was brought out. A copy of a German gun and bayonet was made of wood in the carpentry department. All the Dutchman had to do was to make the prisoners stand at attention inside the gate, count them in good loud German, show papers to the guard at the gate and march the flock out through the gate.

I stood watching them disappear down the road past the old camp. The chief was, however, not satisfied with this. A few minutes after the twenty-five men were out of sight, eight or ten higher officers lined up inside the gate with the camp's adjutant in command. He explained to the guard that they were going over to confer with the German camp commandant, that they were late and the guard would do well to let them out quickly. The inner gate was already open before the German got suspicious.

He went into the guardroom to telephone and get information, after asking the German in the nearest tower to keep an eye on the 'delegation'.

Not many minutes elapsed before the captain in charge of the camp guard drove up. He rubbed his hands, well pleased with his 'catch'. But his pleasure did not last long. A German came running up, all hot and bothered, with the news that twenty-five prisoners had marched out of the camp about a quarter of an hour ago. The captain's colour and expression changed. Then the general alarm went. We stood the whole of that morning and afternoon on the sports ground while the Germans checked every single man in the camp, one by one, to find out who was missing. The check lasted six hours, three hours of which we stood in pouring rain. The German camp leader, an oldish Prussian, almost got a stroke through rage at the thought of the twenty-five who were now walking about in the neighbourhood.

Unfortunately it did not take long before a couple of them were caught and put into prison (fourteen days of bread and water was the reward for an escape attempt). Within the next few days the others were caught and brought back. One Englishman succeeded in getting all the way to the Swiss border but was stopped there at passport control.

The whole camp was punished by having five roll calls per day and searches at night or in the morning before anyone was awake. The night searches were as a rule not very disagreeable. The Germans came in quietly and only counted the prisoners. But the morning visitations were worse. Then they woke us with noise and shouts and we had to hurry into our clothes and get food ready for the day. After a body search we were hounded out of the huts. When we were out, the Germans started rummaging through the rooms. Fortunately they usually went through one hut at a time, and friends always invited us to dinner. Such searches could last four or five hours. The Germans mostly got very meagre results, but went on annoying us in this manner for a couple of weeks before they were through with us. They then returned to their former routine.

Work on the tunnels was started again and sand carriers once more went for walks. The Germans were now, though, aware of the fact that something was brewing and hid behind camouflaged positions outside the fence and use field glasses. The trees in the camp, however, obstructed their view and were removed, much to our disappointment and annoyance. The camp looked cold and naked without trees and the prisoners had now to work much more cautiously. Working tempo decreased again.

All materials and tools used were hidden in the tunnels, and if they had been found and confiscated it would have been nearly impossible to start anything new. The work was therefore stopped for the time being while the committee worked out a plan of action.

It was at this time that the American Air Force was engaged in great strength over Germany during daylight, apparently with heavy losses. When American airmen once started coming to the camp they came in large flocks. The reason for this large number of American prisoners compared with those of the other Allies was chiefly because of the difference between RAF and American fighting tactics. The Americans bombed during day and were therefore heavily attacked by fighter planes. They had to keep in close formation in order to be able to cover each other with machine guns, and in order that their combined defensive fire was as intense as possible. If a bomber was hit or dropped behind it was almost a certain prey for the Germans. American crews therefore had orders to bale out in their parachutes as soon as damage to their plane forced them out of formation and they were attacked by German fighters. This was also why the crews from downed American planes got out alive in forty to fifty per cent of the cases.

RAF planes mostly bombed at night, therefore flew singly and could count on the darkness to help them against night fighter planes. When they were hit by anti-aircraft fire or fighter planes they didn't bale out at once but hoped to get away in the darkness. They did not bale out even if they knew there were fighter planes close by. As a rule the fighter plane which spotted them and shot them down appeared before they had time to bale out. Only fifteen to twenty per cent of the crew from downed RAF bombers escaped alive and became prisoners of war.

The new camp had to date only been half full, but now was becoming full very quickly – as already mentioned, mostly by Americans, but also by RAF personnel. The prisoners from Poland had returned long ago. The two Norwegians who had been there had moved in with us, as arranged, and now we had our own Norwegian room for the first time. The Germans had been building new huts to the south of our camp for a long time. The Americans were to move in there when it was ready. Meantime, our camp soon became full, and some huts had to house many more than they were intended for. It was with mixed feelings that we looked forward to the day when the Americans were to move. It would be sad to part from good friends and a relief to have enough room to move about in.

Americans always brought fun and good humour with them. They had several good amateur actors and musicians among them, who gave us many enjoyable evenings in the theatre, which had been completed some time before the Americans moved into their new camp. We had obtained a whole hut from the Germans for the theatre. Architects among the prisoners planned the building and directed the work. When ready it was a great success. The hall could hold an audience of three to four hundred, and the rows of seats were made of old packing cases. Costumes and make-up were hired from Berlin. Deliveries from there were often delayed, but we gladly excused them, knowing the reason for the delays.

Theatre personnel took their work very seriously and worked long hours with rehearsals and stage equipment. The zeal of those making the scenery, by the way, put a sudden and unexpected stop to an attempt to escape, which probably would otherwise have succeeded.

A wing-commander was the victim of this unfortunate occurrence, a veteran who had won many honours in the Battle of Britain. He was a young man, very self-confident and dignified. He had planned his escape for some time and had chosen a German refuse cart, which drove regularly in and out of the camp, as his conveyance. The cart in question was drawn by one horse and used to come to the camp once or twice a week to empty the camp's garbage bins and fetch empty tins. The driver drove out as soon as he had a full load. This was repeated until all the garbage bins were emptied and tins collected. The driver was a wizened old German civilian. A soldier went with him to see that no one tried to hide in the cart. A couple of English sergeants had the job of shovelling the tins onto the cart. Experience taught us that it was easy enough to distract the attention of the driver and the guard by offering them cigarettes and chatting with them. A man could in the meantime jump into the cart and be covered with tins.

The wing-commander, equipped with everything needed for a trip through Germany, jumped onto the cart one day and was covered with tin cans, according to plan. Everything went well until the driver decided to drive over to the garbage bin placed just outside the theatre. As soon as the cart came to a standstill there a scenery painter came out with a bucket full of old paint and emptied it over the cart load. Onlookers related that the wing-commander let out a yell from the midst of the tin. It must have given the old driver a shock to see a human form rise with paint running from hair, face and clothes. The wing-commander was furious, the painter of scenery most unhappy. The would-be escapee got fourteen days' bread and water and never again tried to escape in a garbage cart.

The weeks passed and 'Tom' had now gone so far that the work-face was under the fence. Then it was discovered.

The Germans were triumphant and blasted the whole thing with dynamite. Like 'Dick' and 'Harry', 'Tom' had been constructed and equipped as solidly as possible. It was completely lined with wooden boards; it had electric light, trolleys running on rails for conveying personnel and sand, and an air pump to pump fresh air into the tunnel. The Germans were impressed and condescendingly complimented the prisoners on their good work. We gathered by what they said that they believed 'Tom' was our only project of this kind. Which suited Big X fine. 'Harry' had progressed furthest, but it was getting so late in the year that it could not be finished before winter and the bad weather set in. Work on 'Dick' and 'Harry' was therefore stopped, and the camp took up more peaceful occupations.

The autumn was eventful. A couple of Poles proved to be experts at distilling alcohol. In the old camp a concoction was sometimes brewed of raisins, sugar and water – a dreadful fluid which, however, made anyone who drank a pint or two of it drunk. One also felt quite ill afterwards. Raisins were soaked in sugar and water and allowed to ferment for a fortnight. When the fermenting was ended the thick mixture was filtered and drunk at a festive occasion.

The Poles improved the production methods. They made distilling apparatus. The thick sour raisin wine was boiled and the alcohol distilled. After a second distilling the alcohol percentage was about sixty. Essences were now made from apricots and prunes. The finished products were good and had the desired effect. Many jolly parties were held that autumn without any unpleasant incidents. One night, though, one of the guests ended up in hospital after a pleasant evening. He forgot, for very good reasons, to go home to his own hut before doors were locked. When at last he decided to go home he had to jump out of a window and landed on all fours. Finding himself in this position he thought it best to continue moving on in the same position. A German dog saw him when he had gone halfway towards his hut. It gave the alarm at once and started attacking him. Our guest stood up on unsteady legs and put up a fight against the dog, trying to move towards his goal. But a German had arrived, pointing a revolver and shouting, 'Halt!' Our friend, being deaf in one ear, simply continued walking. Whereupon the German fired and hit him in the thigh. Only after spending one month in hospital was he able to return home to his hut.

The autumn set in, sharp and cold. But no snow for a long time. After walking the daily rounds one usually sat indoors, reading or writing during the morning, and playing cards or visiting acquaintances in the afternoon and evening. As time went on there were now fourteen Norwegians in the camp. Twelve of us lived together in two rooms. The other two lived in English rooms. There were quarrels once in a while, when a fellow got out of bed on the wrong side, but on the whole we got along well. Everything considered, I am glad to have had this experience.

The work on 'Dick' and 'Harry' was stopped for the time being. But we had enough to do and enough to think about and to plan. Amusing episodes were not wanting either – such as when Jan and an Englishman climbed the fence and disappeared into the forest one fine Sunday afternoon. It was a bold plan. Jan and his comrade would climb the fence between two watchtowers. One of the watchmen was a 'tame' German and well instructed in the part he was to play. The part was easy enough: it was merely to look in the correct direction while the two men climbed over and ran into the forest. The other guard was not on our side, and to distract his attention two prisoners were scheduled to start a fight. I didn't know when the escape would take place, but I happened to be out for a walk just then and saw the whole thing. First a terrific din was heard in the hut where the fight started. The two men who fought played their part well. One of them was thrown against a glass door, so that shards of glass flew. Outside on the ground they rolled over each other in a most realistic struggle. The watchman in the tower was fascinated, as intended. As soon as the guard's interest was established, a sign was given to Jan and the Englishman. They walked quickly out of their hut, over the warning wire, towards the fence, and were over it in no time. Both the guards were still looking in the desired direction. Jan and his friend ran across the road and into the open space before the forest. Then I heard a German call out. It was not one of the guards but someone outside the fence. The tame guard had to turn round. He raised his rifle and shot at the two, who were now running for the woods a few metres away. The guard missed and before he could take aim again the two were out of sight.

In the wood a voice called, 'Halt!' several times and soon afterwards Jan and the Englishman came out onto the road, with a German officer with a pistol behind them. The end of this adventure was fourteen days on bread and water, thanks to the German officer who was taking his Sunday walk in the woods. I don't think anyone had attempted just such an escape before, and no one has since.

A period with thick fog every morning set in. The fog was so thick that one couldn't see from one hut to another. Many cut their way through the fence on such mornings but did not get further than the 'clink'. There was now very little to do in my department and for a time I worked in the tailor shop, where there was always more than enough to do. Arrangements were being made for the day when 'Harry' would be completed. Large numbers of civilian clothes and German uniforms had to be made ready. I was working on my own clothes; Pete, who had a permanent job as tailor, was busy making his own things too.

By the way, Pete got a little 'holiday' for fourteen days that autumn, for going out of camp one evening after dark. Pete had been a student in Germany before the war and spoke the language very well and was given a chance to attempt escape. Dressed as a German who daily patrolled the camp, he sauntered out of the camp when the guards were changing. All went well until a German guard who was going the same way and wanted company found out that something was wrong. They walked along together for a while but the German finally grew suspicious and Pete was nabbed.

The frost set in. We were provided with fuel for our stoves. We hoped it would be so cold that we could make a skating rink. But the weather was unsettled. It would freeze for a whole week so the ice got harder and thick. Then a change came before we could use it. We were obliged to stop walking rounds along the fence earlier and earlier every evening. We were only allowed to walk between the huts until the doors were locked at ten o'clock. We heard bombing attacks on Berlin and Dresden much more often now. Planes often flew so near our camp that all lights had to be put out and we were left in total darkness. Sometimes explosions were so heavy that the frozen ground transmitted the vibrations from more than 160 kilometres away and shook our window panes. Many prisoners waited and hoped for those nights when all lights in the camp were put out. But the Germans had learned to be more watchful. On such nights they redoubled their patrols outside the fence and used dogs.

Soon snow began to fall. At first a few inches of moist snow, then dry snow. This snow warmed up the camp. Dust was laid, and the snow against the huts protected against draughts and the cold ground

Then Christmas came, and we had a happy time. Food was better and more plentiful than the first Christmas. News from England was good and gave us hope. A special department listened in on the news, copied it down at night and read it in the huts next day.

When the New Year festivities were over, Big X decided the time was ripe to start serious work again. All efforts should be centred on completing 'Harry'. In spite of the snow, work was started. During the long winter months this last great effort had been planned down to the minutest details, and a good deal of preliminary work done.

The main task was to dig the last seventy metres so quickly that even if the Germans suspected something was brewing they would not take action and come down on us before it was too late.

As long as there was snow on the ground the sand which was brought out from 'Harry' obviously could not be spread out on the roads and paths of the camp. It would have to be dispersed in some other way.

At first the sand was to be carried down into 'Dick'. Only thirty metres of 'Dick' was dug, and this had been used as a storing place for tools, clothes and other equipment. When 'Dick' was full, the rest of the sand would be thrown under the theatre building. For some reason the Germans did not suspect that this building was being used for anything which was 'Verboten'.

The work was started, and within a week everything was running according to schedule. The tunnel progressed with a hitherto unprecedented speed. The digging was only interrupted a couple of times in order to test and service the air pump and trolleys.

The digging shifts went down as soon as the morning roll call at ten o'clock was over. The entrance was then closed. The sand which they dug out was driven right back to the entrance shaft. It was stored there in sacks in a special room. The first shift worked below until the afternoon roll call at four o'clock. After this roll call the entrance was once again opened and the bags of sand hauled up and hidden in rooms in the huts. The entrance was again closed and the sand carriers started their walk – at first between the tunnel hut and 'Dick', later between the tunnel hut and the theatre. Traffic was directed by several routes in order that the procession of sand carriers would not be too obvious.

The atmosphere in the camp grew more and more tense as the days and weeks went by. It was not yet decided who should go out through 'Harry'. Those who could speak German were certain of getting the chance.

All who thought they had a chance of going out were putting finishing touches on plans for their trip through Germany. Then one day lots were drawn. One hundred and fifty names were taken out of a tin box. Pete, Haldor, Nils and I were among the lucky ones.* We could all speak German and also had the advantage of being Norwegians and could play the part of Norwegian volunteer labourers. Photographs of us for our false papers were taken with a camera 'borrowed' from a German officer while he was watching a performance at our theatre.

Those who received good papers had to back these with a credible story in case they were cross-examined on the way. Our last weeks were devoted to working out all the details of the story and to putting finishing touches to our equipment.

---

* Nils Jørgen Fuglesang, the fourth Norwegian to escape. He was captured together with Espelid near Flensburg close to the Danish border, and was later shot.

The Last Days

During the last week before 24 March 1944 the atmosphere in the camp was tense, to say the least. 'Harry' was ready and only some minor adjustments would be made on the morning of the day of action. During this last week the leaders had picked out or chosen those who were to escape, and each person was given a turn number. I got number 13 and Pete number 14. We were all given orders to complete our equipment and wait in readiness.

The whole camp was in a state of intense but hidden activity. Especially those working in the clothes and papers departments were more or less in a flat spin because they were short of time. A number of small meetings were held in the huts, where the different specialists gave advice and made suggestions as to how we should cope with the main problems and difficulties which could crop up on the way.

It so happened that Pete and I both decided to go to Stettin, so we made up a common scheme and went to the 'map department' together. We were to impersonate Norwegian electricians who had taken work in Germany in accordance with the organization of voluntary labour, and we concocted a story along these lines. We worked out all the details and left the rest to the 'papers department'. They went around the camp to gather the necessary data, make suggestions and give advice. Tim was the chief of this department. His work had stood its test time and again and proved to be almost perfect in every detail. We therefore felt that this preparatory work was in the best hands.

As far as clothes and luggage were concerned (both were very important as we were to travel by train and had to look fairly decent), my equipment was ready. The only thing left was to press my suit.

My suit consisted of an RAF airman's tunic, which had been closely shaved, making the material's weaving show clearly. This changed the look of the jacket very much. Then the cut was changed to make the jacket look like a single-breasted civilian one. Thirdly, the tailors had dyed it dark blue and sewn on civilian buttons. When it was pressed it didn't look so bad. The trousers were genuine grey civilian flannel ones which happened to have passed the German control. A dark-grey Italian army shirt and a tie made out of the leg of old pyjamas, a Canadian knitted lumber jacket and a pair of American military boots completed the outfit. Pete looked like a king compared to me. He had a complete dark-blue naval uniform which had been altered where necessary. On top of this he used his own RAF uniform coat. The cut was not changed at all, only the buttons were covered with leather procured from some old boxing gloves. We were each to carry a small case containing things necessary for a normal two-day journey.

Those of us who were going out through 'Harry' at first thought we would have our hands full getting ready, but there was still lots of time left over to sit and wait for orders; and to build up a gnawing feeling of tension.

The orders we received came from a 'marshal'. This man had to see that the small group of prisoners in his care got all the help they needed before going out through the tunnel. Thus the fugitives could simply sit down and tell him what they needed and if this was within reason it was procured.

On the morning of 24 March our marshal came and gave us the code words: 'Tonight's the night.'

I had waited for this a long time and was prepared for it; still, when I heard it a cold shiver ran down my back. During the day I noticed a new, tense and expectant expression on the faces of my companions. The thought of leaving this hated god-forsaken place made us go about as if in a dream. But, at the same time, we felt relieved. After the intense period of waiting and preparation it was good to know at last that now it was going to happen, and to concentrate on it.

There were many more smiling faces to be seen about than usual. But of course there were those whose preparations were not yet complete and their faces did not look exactly peaceful. I myself was getting a sixpence cap ready.

After lunch we received our papers. I had expected them to be well made out, but had never dreamed they would be so perfect. Even though I knew that each of the five papers I received was false and made by hand I could scarcely detect the forgery.

Tim, chief of the papers department, came himself and explained to us how the papers would work. He spoke fast and concisely and then went on to the next group.

I was a Norwegian workman, an electrician employed by A/G Siemens Bauunion, Frankfurt an der Oder. On 19 June 1943 I had come to Germany as a volunteer and had then lived in a workmen's camp in Frankfurt. As we were going to Stettin through Frankfurt, a difficulty arose at once – a weak point in our story. If our papers were checked on the way between Sagan (where we were now) and Frankfurt, it would be difficult to explain why we were going to Stettin when we lived in a worker's camp in Frankfurt. Two different stories had therefore been made up. One was to be used if we were stopped and checked between Sagan and Frankfurt, the other one between Frankfurt and Stettin. The first story stated that Siemens had sent us on a special job to install some transformers at a power station in one of the small towns near Sagan, and we were now returning to Frankfurt. This story was weak. If we ran into a zealous controller we had to be prepared to be cross-examined on this point; we had to come up with the name of the village, the power station's exact address, the names of those we had spoken to there, etc. But we decided to take the risk. It was in reality not so great because we were going to travel to Frankfurt by ordinary passenger train, where there was usually no check. I shall come back to the story to be told on the journey from Frankfurt to Stettin. I had perhaps better start by describing our papers.

The most important one was an identity paper issued by the workers' camp at Frankfurt an der Oder. A photo of the holder was attached to this paper and stated that he had permission to work and to remain on government property, including railway yards, dockyards and such like. In short, places where it was forbidden for ordinary civilians – even German workmen – to be. We hoped this would help if we were found on some fenced-off dock while looking for a steamer to board. It could also happen that we got into some difficult situation where we would have to hide in a freight car. If found in a railway yard, we had this paper to show. We would show this paper first under any circumstances if we met an inspector. Our identity papers were also a masterpiece. One thing was missing, however: namely the decision of what our nationality was to be. This had to be added on a typewritten slip of paper, stamped by the Berlin police, by the chief of the workers' camp and by Siemens. It was stamped all over in different colours and with important-looking, confidence-inspiring, signatures which were all difficult to decipher. In addition to these two papers we had one made out by the police in Frankfurt. It was permission to travel from Frankfurt to a village an hour's walk from Sagan, to install a transformer in the local power station. As already mentioned, this part of our story could not be made up into a wholly feasible explanation, and therefore this 'travel permit' was to be used only in a tight spot. It was to be destroyed as soon as we arrived in Frankfurt.

We were to make use of two other papers only after our arrival in Frankfurt, and these were meant as a supplement to our story when travelling between Frankfurt and Stettin. These two papers were: (a) a letter from A/G Siemens, written on the firm's own notepaper and headed 'To whom it may concern'. The letter stated that we were transferred to Stettin by the German government to undertake some special work there. And (b) a letter from the workers' camp in Frankfurt addressed 'To whom it may concern' (a common German formula), explaining that we had orders to travel by the shortest route to Stettin and to report to the Bureau of Workers there. At the same time it asked everyone to help us as much as possible. This sounded all right. Besides these solid papers we were each given 160 Reichsmarks for expenses on the journey. We felt very confident and well equipped.

The only thing which brought some doubt was that Tim had not succeeded in procuring some bona fide ration cards. We had heard that civilian travellers who did not have their ration cards with them ran the risk of being arrested. Therefore it was not strange that we felt somewhat uneasy on this point. However, we made up a feasible story to cover this deficiency.

We finally spent much time rehearsing our stories now they were complete. They all seemed to be plausible. Then we turned to perfecting our equipment. During the afternoon on the day of action those occupying the 'action hut' received orders to evacuate it and to go to rooms in the other huts which had been allotted to them earlier.

During the evening those who were going to escape arrived in the 'action hut' one by one. First those whose equipment was not so conspicuous as to reveal their intentions. Later on, as it drew near to closing-up time, many strange apparitions emerged out of the darkness. Those were the 'tough guys', who were going to get through on foot. Some of them had quite fantastic equipment. A few were in full airman's uniform, and most of them were wearing belts of every description, with tin boxes of food fastened to them. Many of them looked grotesque when rigged in full kit. We laughed and made fun of them, little knowing what tragedy this attempt at escape from the German prison camp would end in.

The dimensions of the tunnel made it impossible to wear a lot of clothes or to carry much bulky equipment, and the marshals ordered clothing or equipment which would impede a rapid passage to be taken off. Such equipment had either to be changed or left behind. The latter option was not agreeable as each man had figured out what was absolutely strictly needed. But, as mentioned, each was examined as though they were a loaded freight train, and in many cases radical last-minute changes had to be made.

Thus the last hours in the 'action hut' were marked by a nervous and feverish activity. Fellows taking things off, putting things on, fastening food tins securely in other places than they had done at first, fellows studying maps, men who played cards or the gramophone, and others who were simply sleeping. Some stared into space biting their nails, others worked at crossword puzzles. One could just sit and watch the others if one had nothing better to do. This was sufficient entertainment. I still sat working on my cap. 'Pop' Green, the keenest and most passionate crossword puzzle solver I had ever met, was doing a puzzle and was dead to the world. Then he suddenly looked up. The leader of the whole venture came into the room.

There was complete silence. Everyone looked at this man who had planned and organized the whole thing. We expected him to say something. He merely said: 'Good luck, boys.' And he left.

Rumours went about that the first ones were already on their way out of the tunnel. I believe they started at 22.15 – that is, as soon as the doors of the hut were closed.

The activity of the escapers continued after closing-up time, but now the corridor was also beginning to be full of people. A table was carried out and the chief marshal established his office there. His job was to keep order in the 'road' and regulate the traffic. There were many delays and obstructions on the way out on account of the bulk of some of the 'hikers'.

The hours went by and I sat waiting. The tension was unbearable. It *could* happen that they found us out, as so often before. Perhaps at this very moment a German was standing outside the door of the hut, searching for the key to get in. But our watchmen were out there and our signalling system perfect.

It was 12.30 before Pete and I, numbers 14 and 13 respectively, were ordered into the corridor to stand in readiness to go down the shaft. Those who were still in their rooms at twelve o'clock, when all lights went out, had been told to turn in. Boots and equipment remained in the corridor, to avoid rummaging and noise in the dark rooms. The atmosphere was charged with excitement, the marshals' low-toned orders and quick, stealthy footsteps going back and forth along the corridor did not relieve the tension. The marshals were by this time short-tempered and got worked up at the slightest impediment to traffic through the tunnel. Orders were given that those who were found to be overloaded and too bulky after the last check would be stopped from going through.

Pete and I sat quite close to the door leading into the room where the shaft was. One by one men disappeared through the door, but we could not see the room from where we sat. Something started gnawing at my midrift. I could hardly sit still. At last my turn came. I got up and went through the door. Four cupboards stood in front of the windows so the light from the kerosene lamps would not be seen outside. The shaft led down from one corner of the room. The marshal checked my kit for the last time. All day they had been considering my suitcase and wondering if I could take it through with me. But I climbed down the ladder with the suitcase on my shoulder and noticed nothing wrong. Three men were waiting at the bottom of the shaft, so I had to hang onto the ladder before going all the way down. Then I was told to wait in the discharge room, and this took a couple of minutes. My stomach had quietened. I was no longer nervous. The trolley returned. I put my suitcase in front, on the trolley rails, crawled on behind and wriggled into place. A few seconds later I lay comfortably on my stomach on the trolley, grabbed the suitcase with outstretched arms and lifted it in front of me. Then I ducked my head and gave the 'all clear' signal.

The trolley started to move slowly forwards along the rails. 'The man pulling the rope must be tired now,' I thought. Birkland was pulling it. He had already pulled through twenty of his comrades. I shall never forget him. They shot him shortly after he was caught. At the changeover point, or midway house, he took my suitcase and pushed it forwards into the next tunnel. As I passed him he wished me luck.

The next trolley had not arrived. I pulled the rope and it soon came into view. I lay down on it, my suitcase in front of me in outstretched arms, and soon it started moving. It moved slowly as that part of the tunnel sloped upwards. I didn't know the man pulling this trolley, but he was evidently quite exhausted, the perspiration poured from him, and I wondered how he would feel coming out into the cold air later on. This trolley led right to the bottom of the exit shaft, outside the camp. The manner in which we were to leave the shaft had been changed a little since the whole scheme had been last explained to us, and the new procedure was posted up on the wall of the shaft. Between the end of the trolley rails and the bottom of the shaft there was an opening which was covered with a blanket on account of the blackout. I was determined to take as short a time possible to get through and out, because of the fuss and bother I had had with my suitcase, and in my hurry had pulled the blackout curtain halfway down. I fumbled a bit when getting it in place again. Well, I had made relatively good time. My train was not scheduled to leave for an hour and a half. Apparently the length of the tunnel had been miscalculated to the extent that the exit shaft had surfaced just short of the treeline and not well into the woods as intended. Therefore each man would be plainly visible as he emerged and ran across the open area which separated him from the shelter of the trees.

This danger made it necessary to post a marshal outside to tell each escapee when the coast was clear. The marshal was posted just within the trees. He could signal to the tunnel exit by means of a thin rope laid out on the ground. Before emerging from the shaft, each escapee would tell the marshal 'I'm here' with one pull on the rope. The marshal would then signal back 'Wait' or 'All clear', according to the movements of the Germans.

I lifted the suitcase onto my shoulder and began climbing up the ladder. This shaft was narrower than the descent in the hut but I managed to get out of it without a hitch. Just before reaching the top I spotted the signalling rope, which was fastened to one of the top rungs. I grabbed the rope and pulled it. Waited for an answer but got none. I pulled again and this time received a reply: 'All clear'.

I could see the clear sky above me and small stars indistinctly through the night mist. I climbed up and found my head was above ground. I turned towards the camp and was startled: one of the watchtowers was no more than thirty metres away. The watchman up there was apparently very keen, because he kept on looking in the direction of the camp. As long as he did this we could feel safe. I crawled right up onto the snow-covered ground, and with the guiding rope in my hand walked quickly into the woods.

The rope was only some twenty-five yards long. At the end of it and well into the woods I stopped, turned towards the camp, and with one eye on the watchman began brushing my hair and clothes, which were full of sand.

I felt as though many hours passed before Pete came up out of the shaft and over to me. We saw them changing guards. Twelve Germans marched past on the road, not many metres away from the shaft. We had some tense seconds, but they saw nothing.

Pete also brushed himself and we checked each other's equipment. After a short discussion we decided to walk to the station and find a certain passageway under the rails. This passage should be fairly clear – almost half a kilometre nearer than the next chance of getting across the railway line, which was fenced in. The other possibility was a footbridge over the railway.

We walked slowly along the narrow path in the woods and soon came to a broader road. We turned to the left there and saw the railway station right opposite us. We had not yet met a single person, except one of our comrades, who took another path through the woods.

We walked close to the fence beside the railway line. We looked in vain for the underground passage. Then we turned and walked back the same way and at last found it. We saw a sign: 'For Wehrmacht use only'. We decided to use the bridge for pedestrians and walked down beside the fence. We arrived at a storage yard for timber that had large stacks of planks in rows. We stopped. This yard was very large. We decided to walk right through it instead of sneaking around it and went in through the gate. Talking, we marched in between the stacks and in a few minutes were on the other side. Here we could see the bridge we were to cross. So far we had not seen anyone near the station. It seemed as though no one was out so late at night. We hoped the police guard at the station was not posted right in front of the railway station, and walked up the bridge. Our footsteps could surely have been heard many miles away. Down the other side, and towards the station. No policeman. Well, we carried on.

I walked into the hall to buy a ticket. Pete had dropped behind a little. I saw a girl through the aperture and tried to signal to her that I wanted to buy a ticket. But she didn't understand, and I thought I had come to the wrong place. At that moment a German officer entered and, just as I was leaving I saw the girl come up to the counter and open the small window. He asked for a ticket, paid and left.

Pete came in just then. He went to the window and bought two tickets. Then we went out of the hall onto the poorly lit platform, through the enclosure, and stood at last on the platform from which our train would leave, the train which would take us from Sagan, where we were, to Frankfurt an der Oder.

There were a number of people on the platform in spite of the early hour. Personally, I did not feel at ease. I felt as though everyone turned to stare at us. It took some minutes for me to realize that this was not the case. People of all nationalities walked up and down the platforms or stood chatting together in small groups. We were not in immediate danger of being discovered.

According to the schedule, the train was to leave at three minutes past two, and to our astonishment it puffed into the station just before two o'clock. We managed to squeeze into a third-class compartment. There was no light in the carriage, but in the dim blueish light on the platform and station we could discern our fellow travellers. From what we could see and from what we could hear of their conversation we understood that most of them were Polish or Czech workmen. Most of them sat slumped down on the benches and slept. Some sat on suitcases or parcels in the corridor. The train seemed to be quite full. Anyway, our compartment was crowded.

Suddenly the train started to move. We were on our way home! Through the door leading to the corridor we could hear people talking and laughing in the adjoining compartment. They seemed to be soldiers and young girls. The train increased its speed and soon went quite fast. We soon found, however, that we were not on an express train. It stopped at every small station. At one of the stations a woman with a pram boarded the train. There were two children in it. They looked all right but the mother seemed very nervous and anxious after the job of getting onto the train. She was very conscious of being a good German mother, and in an authoritative voice ordered those in the compartment to make room for her and the youngsters. Gradually she calmed down, and after two hours looked as though she would fall asleep. Daylight was creeping in. My thoughts went back to the camp. The tunnel would surely be cleared now, since the shaft would show against the snow. I sincerely hoped it had not been discovered at that time. But while I sat there in the train I did not know that out of the eighty-two men who succeeded in getting through the tunnel* before daylight only three of them were to get out of Germany and back to England. Birkland, who had pulled us through the tunnel, was one

---

* There were actually eighty-three men who made it down the shaft: four were caught at the tunnel entrance, three were apprehended at the tunnel exit, which meant seventy-six successfully cleared the tunnel and made their escape. Seventy-three were subsequently captured at various locations, of whom fifty were executed and only twenty-three returned to the camp.

of those who did not get back. He and fifty-four others were shot after they were caught in different parts of Germany. Only three of us had good luck.

As we rumbled along I was half expecting a train search to take place at any moment. The tunnel could have been discovered and the police alarmed for miles around. Our journey would then come to an abrupt end. But – we arrived at Frankfurt without any mishap.

At six o'clock in the morning we stepped out onto the platform and walked towards the ticket inspector. This was another tense moment, but we got through without any fuss and were soon afterwards in the waiting room finding out when the train would leave for our next destination. We could choose between two trains. One went directly to Stettin, and the other to Kustrin,* where it connected very nicely with a train to Stettin. The first one, which went straight to Stettin, was an ordinary slow passenger train, and there was very rarely inspection of any kind on these slow trains. However, it did not leave until late in the afternoon. Therefore we decided to take the one going to Kustrin, although this was an express train, with frequent inspections.

We bought tickets and now had over an hour at our disposal before the train left. We walked about the town, but felt uneasy, since the streets were deserted at this early hour. We were glad to get back to the station.

---

* Now Kostrzyn nad Odrą.

The train left punctually and after a two-hour journey without excitement of any kind we arrived at Kustrin, a large railway junction.

It was nine o'clock. If everything in the camp had run according to schedule the tunnel would not yet have been discovered, and we would be safe for about another hour. But at the morning roll call at ten o'clock the escape would be discovered, the alarm would go and then we could meet with difficulties at any moment. We would then be on our train to Stettin.

We were hungry and went into the waiting room after first checking and finding that departure would be in about an hour's time. So at ten o'clock we would still be in the station at Kustrin and not on the train. We looked for seats in the waiting room. The room was crowded but we found an empty table which some German soldiers had just left. We sat down, took out our sandwiches, ordered some beer and started to enjoy our breakfast. Pete made a sign to me to turn round and look towards the door. I did so. Two friends from the camp entered the room. They looked about, and as there were some other empty seats at our table, came up to us and sat down. We pretended not to know them. They ordered beer, but soon got up and left the table. They smiled slightly as they left and so did we – Good luck!

The time passed slowly. The room was crowded with all sorts of people, soldiers and civilians. We had finished eating and sat watching the people and chatting, when Pete stopped suddenly in the middle of a sentence. He looked towards the exit, turned his head calmly my way and said, 'Don't turn round. An inspector is coming towards us.'

He stubbed out his cigarette. I heard footsteps behind me, boots. They stopped. Pete looked up, past me. I heard a commanding German voice:

'Papers, please.'

I turned round and saw a young German with a sharp face and hard eyes. Pete took out his pocket book. I did the same. I tried to keep my hand from trembling as I handed him my papers. He looked at me.

'Soldiers?' he asked.

'No,' we answered. 'Norwegian workmen.' He looked at us again and we at him. Then he read our papers. Stood without saying a word. Only read on. He looked efficient. Was the tunnel discovered? Pete and I exchanged glances.

Then again we heard the German. 'Good.' He handed us our papers, saluted and left.

We breathed more easily. But the air in the waiting room felt stifling. It was better out on the platform. As we got up to walk across the room, we saw the German right in front of us. He stared at me and looked at me inquiringly while we walked up to him and past him.

The two comrades we had met in the waiting room were to take another train. They were probably going to Danzig. Later on we heard that two had boarded a freight ship as stowaways. Out at sea they had given themselves up to the captain. This fellow had turned the ship round, gone back to Danzig and given the fugitives up to the German authorities. They were shot.

I asked Pete to wait on the platform while I went to the toilet. When I came out again he had disappeared. I waited a while. Then I thought perhaps he had gone over to the platform from where the train would leave, and I went there. But no Pete to be seen. I would not walk back again as he could very well have been arrested. Perhaps they were also looking for me. The train had come in and would be leaving in a few minutes. Then I caught sight of Pete. I saw him coming out of a dark corner just as the train was about to start. He said he had hidden there out of the way of the German inspector.

We boarded the train. It was almost empty. For quite some time we had the compartment to ourselves. Even with the worst part of our journey still before us we were glad to leave Kustrin.

The train jogged along. We were quite sure the escape had been discovered, but the chances of an inspection on this train were small. The only check would be when our tickets were taken at the exit from the station.

Stettin

I felt uneasy on leaving the train at Stettin, but nothing happened. We walked past the ticket collector without trouble and soon stood on the street outside the station.

It was about one o'clock and we had several hours to kill before we could call at the address given to us in the camp. We decided to walk along the river and down to the harbour. We tried to recall streets, bridges and districts we had seen on maps in the camp. We walked on thus for two hours and at last reached the business area of the town. The RAF had evidently taken a dislike to the business area of Stettin. There was very little of it left.

We walked down a street leading to the railway station called Grune Schantze. We saw a pub there and went in, hoping to get a meal without ration points. We soon found that the only thing we could get there was thin beer. We ordered thin beer. Two large Seidels, which we drank very slowly. When they were finished we ordered two more. I sat for quite a while watching a fat girl consume a large bowl of vegetable soup. Then we felt that if we sat too long over our beer someone there might start wondering what we were doing. We got up and went out again into the street.

We wandered about without any definite goal and soon came to a cinema. This was actually what we needed. The film was worse than we expected, but it helped us to while away two hours.

Now it was a little after five and time to look for our contact address and the street number before it got too dark. We walked along on the pavement and stopped a small boy. Asked him where Klein-Oder Strasse was. We knew that this was a notorious street. The lad showed us the way.

We found the street and the number. The place looked dead. We walked slowly past the house and continued along the pavement. It would soon be dark, and we had not gone far before we thought it safest to turn and walk back again. It was dark when we again passed the house.

Now the street was no longer empty. We saw the dark figures of men standing talking to each other in muffled tones, people walking up and down the pavement, and men going from one group to another. We could dimly see dozens of them in the semi-darkness. Presently we found the number we were looking for. The door was locked. I knocked. We waited, listening intently. I knocked again. We did not hear a sound inside. I began to lose patience. Then one of the figures came up to us and asked in broken German what we wanted. I stood considering what to answer when he asked me if I had something to sell. I said no, and that I was looking for a brothel. Our intention was first of all to make contact with the girls in the brothel, as this was the address given us in the camp. Then we would persuade or bribe them to hide us until we could get in touch with a sailor from a Swedish boat. Meantime Pete used his imagination. He understood that the man was a black-marketeer on the lookout for something to buy or to exchange. Pete showed him some tobacco and asked for bread coupons. The man disappeared and soon returned with bread coupons for two kilos of bread. Pete got another kilo in exchange for his old pullover.

We asked if he knew any Swedish seamen. 'Sure! – Komm mit,' he said, and started to walk. We followed. He stopped in front of the house next to ours and asked us to wait. He went in and came out at once with another shadow who turned out to be a Finn. He spoke Swedish, and on hearing our request went out into the darkness and brought back a Swede.

We took the Swede aside, told him our whole story and asked him to help us. It seemed to amuse him and without hesitation he agreed to smuggle us on board the ship he was on. It was going to Gothenburg the next morning at four o'clock. He asked us to come back at ten o'clock and he would show us the way.

Well, we had some hours at our disposal and walked about the streets to pass the time. We soon came to a pub, went in and ordered beer. We also ate up the remaining food we had with us. We sat there as long as possible, but after a while felt people were staring at us and thought it best to leave.

The next place we visited was a wine bar. There was not much wine to be had there so we again ordered beer and stood talking to the owner for over an hour. Pete talked. Once I forgot myself and said some words in English. The man didn't notice this, only went on talking – it was a most entertaining hour. The German had a map of England on the wall behind the counter, and once in a while gave it a good kick with his heel. The map was full of kick marks. It gave him a certain satisfaction to do this. He was very afraid of the Russians. But the time had passed and we left the place. Out in the dark street we made our way slowly towards Klein-Oder Strasse. We arrived there at least one hour too early and waited for the Swede.

Pete went inside to look for him. I waited. Now a crowd of men were standing in front of the house. But not anywhere else in the street. Pete came out.

'I have found the address,' he said. 'It is number 17. They gave us the wrong number.'

The brothel we were to go to was in number 17 and not in number 16 as we had been told. We went in. The place was run by French and Czech girls and was reserved for foreigners. Business seemed to be flourishing.

The waiting room was crowded, mostly with young boys who awaited their 'turn'. A slender young Czech girl went from one to the other, chatting, laughing and telling sexy stories – evidently to keep the boys warmed up. And she seemed to know each one personally.

Our Swede was in here too. He was standing just inside the door. We stood watching this strange scene, then he asked us to follow him. We left our suitcases in the 'waiting room'. They would be in the way if we got into a tight spot. We walked along Klein-Oder Strasse towards the railway station. After walking two blocks we turned to the left and continued until we came to the street running beside the river, the same one we had walked along in the morning. We crossed over the first bridge we came to. For some minutes we walked through dark streets, and then the Swede suddenly stopped outside a small café. He said he wanted a drink. OK, we said, and went in after him. But we were scarcely seated at the table when air-raid sirens began howling.

Everyone in the room ran out into the street to find a shelter and we ran with the crowd. The Swede led the way through the dark streets at a quick pace. We arrived shortly afterwards at an open place, then turned off to the left and were soon standing before a huge iron gate. It was the entrance to the quay where the boat was lying.

Our guide took out his papers and made a signal to us to follow him. He walked towards the gate, fumbled a little in the dark as though looking for the entrance to the guardroom where the harbour police were checking all who went in and out. But instead of going into the guardroom the Swede pushed open the iron gate just a wee bit and sneaked through. With his torchlight he showed us a chain and told us to crawl under it and inside. Then he disappeared in the dark.

People behind us were hurrying to the shelter, but we could only hear them. Pete and I bent down and crawled quickly under the chain. We then looked about us to get our bearings and walked forwards gingerly. We passed the end of the guardroom and heard a German call out to us. It startled us, but he only asked us to walk faster, which we did willingly.

After a short distance we stopped to wait for the Swede. We could hear police calling to people to hurry up. Planes could be there at any moment. Then we heard someone whistle softly. We stood still. The signal came again and we whistled back. Shortly afterwards our friend came towards us in the dark and whispered to us to follow him.

Thus we continued on our road to freedom. We walked towards the quay, past some ships lying at anchor. Most of them were German. I did not hear any planes. The Swede led the way in between some railway carriages, then went on slowly and cautiously. Shortly afterwards he stopped, turned towards us and asked us to wait until he gave us a signal that we could follow him. He wanted to go on board the ship alone to see if the coast was clear.

He disappeared and we were left on our own. He had told us that it was now up to us to get on board the ship. It would be too dangerous for him to accompany us.

Pete and I hid in the dark under one of the freight cars, peering into the night and listening for any suspicious noises or lights from guards or inspectors. Several times we thought we heard the signal from the Swede, but found it was only imagination. We could make out very indistinctly the shape of a couple of small steamers lying at the quay but did not know which one the Swede had boarded. Time seemed long. We heard voices – German. And soon afterwards we heard footsteps approaching. We looked in the direction of the noise. Iron-heeled boots tramped against the cobblestones. Just as they passed us, only a few feet away, someone lit his torch to look at his watch. They were three policemen. The light went out and the sound of their footsteps faded in the distance.

When we had been thus hiding for a quarter of an hour or so one of the ships left and glided out of the harbour. The hours passed, and slowly it dawned on us that the steamer which left must have been the Swedish one. Damn it ! Still, this was only our first attempt. We decided to find an empty box car and get some sleep there before returning to the streets. We found a freight car and crept into it as noiselessly as possible. We needed sleep. It was cold and I was not warmly dressed. Neither was Pete, but we tried to keep one another warm and fell asleep. While I was half asleep I heard voices and opened my eyes. I woke Pete and we listened to the voices. We were shivering with cold. The voices died away and once more we breathed easily. Our arms and legs were stiff from the cold and the uncomfortable position we had been sitting in. Impossible to sleep any more.

It was now about three in the morning and we decided to leave the docks and return to town. We waited and listened a long while before opening the door and jumping out of the car. Then we walked towards the gate without trying to soften our footsteps. We passed many large ships and noticed the name of the largest: 'Main'. If asked we could say we had just done some work on board her.

Shortly afterwards we met a watchman. 'Guten abend,' I said, and he answered, 'Guten morgen.'

Nothing exciting happened and we reached the gate. We walked through the guardroom and tried to get out but the door was locked. Then we decided to trust to our papers and walked straight into the lighted watchroom. An old night-watchman answered 'Good morning' to my greeting and asked to see papers when we said we were going out. We gave them to him and my heart pounded while he looked at them. He looked at me and asked where we had been working. I answered 'Main'. That was OK. He returned our papers, walked us to the big gate and unlocked it. Much relieved, we went through the gate in the dim morning light.

Klein-Oder Strasse 17 was closed, and we tried all the doors hoping someone would give us a bed or somewhere to sleep. But no one came and we had no choice but to walk about the streets. It was tiring walking up and down streets at a not too suspiciously slow pace, so we took a tramcar and travelled on it to the outskirts of the town. There we found a railway restaurant, went in, bought bread with ration coupons and ordered coffee.

An hour later we were again walking the streets. Now there were people about but still we walked fast so as not to be noticed in the hurry and bustle about us. We decided to find a hotel where we could sleep after our night in the freight car. After looking at a couple of places we decided on one. We drank a glass of beer in the restaurant before renting a room. The place was full of people and we seemed to attract attention. We were taken to the proprietor who sat at one of the tables. He was a stout man and looked at us suspiciously when we asked for a room. However, he agreed to let us have one for the day. First, however, he wanted to see our papers. By now I trusted them implicitly and showed them to him without hesitation. The proprietor looked at them and carefully asked us a few questions. He was not quite sure – had never seen such papers before. But he looked respectfully at all the stamps and signatures and was probably afraid of making a fool of himself by asking too much. We were evidently important persons, according to our papers, and he gave orders to take us to a room.

We went straight to bed after asking to be called at five o'clock. This would be the right time to start looking for a new Swede. I fell asleep at once, but strangely enough woke up at 4.30 a.m.

We dressed, paid the bill and left the hotel. Then we took the shortest route to Klein-Oder Strasse and arrived at number 17 around six o'clock. It was quite light and the streets were empty. Just then two civilians passed us and I thought I heard one of them speaking Swedish. We followed them at once and asked them to stop. Yes, they were Swedish sailors. We asked them to help us. Our story was soon told and they both decided just as quickly. Without wasting a minute, we started out towards their ship. First by tramcar eastwards. The quay was some distance. Our new friends did not know how far we had to travel and we got out one stop after the correct one. We had to walk back over a small bridge. Right in the middle of it stood a police guard. He asked to see our papers. The two Swedes took out theirs and showed them to him, and Pete and I were about to do the same when the policeman waved us all on. He assumed we were all of one crew and allowed us to pass.

We turned off the main street and started walking in a northerly direction, talking all the while about how we should get on board. At first we agreed that the Swedes were to go on board and get papers belonging to two of their comrades while Pete and I hid nearby. They would then come back with the papers, and with these we hoped to get through the inspection at the quay. Pete and I showed them our own papers which had done such good service, and we suggested that the Swedes could tell the guard that we were two old friends they had met and now wished to invite on board for a couple of hours. If this did not work and we were still free we could get the borrowed papers and use them as soon as the guard changed.

After a few minutes' quick walk we arrived at the quay and found the ship among many others moored there. The German guard near the ship stood in deep conversation with a friend. He also found it necessary to inspect only the Swedes' papers. Pete and I followed them closely and he merely waved us on. We went on board and down to the forward crew cabin.

Our two friends' cabin was small but clean and cosy. One of them disappeared and soon returned with food and beer. White bread, real butter and smoked sausage, to say nothing of Swedish export beer. It tasted heavenly. We sat talking and eating for over an hour. It was then time for Pete and me to hide. Our two friends were afraid some other members of the crew would see us and report us to the captain. They did not trust the captain. The result was that we were shown to the place where Pete and I were to spend many long hours, and to experience the most enervating period of our whole escape.

One of them opened the door onto the corridor and peeped out, up and down the passage. He gave the 'all clear' signal to the other man, who quickly bent down and removed a carpet from the floor. There was a hatchway in the iron deck. He opened it and a black hole with a small ladder became visible. He crept down the ladder and disappeared. A moment later he reappeared and indicated to us to follow him. Pete and I went down the ladder. It was cold and damp down there. The Swede had a torch. We stood with our backs to the bow of the ship, and one yard in front was the bulkhead of the compartment for the anchor chains. This bulkhead was made of iron plates. It stretched right across the room and was about five feet high. Six feet further on was another bulkhead. When we stretched up on our toes we could see down into the chain compartments, which were the two centre ones of four such compartments. The two outer ones were only used to store rubbish in. To the left was a huge water tank, taking up almost the whole height of the room. Only one foot separated it from the ceiling and a few inches from the floor. The tank was set up parallel with the chain case bulkhead – that is to say at an angle with the side of the ship, and at the back of it was a dark corner.

At first we saw fit to hide in this corner, behind the water tank. The only approach was to climb onto the chain case, over the bulkhead, down into the rubbish room, over another bulkhead, and down into the corner behind the tank. We did this, rubbing a good deal of skin off our legs. The corner was not as large as it had seemed at first. I especially thought so, being six feet two in stocking feet. But we crept into the hole, and when we had settled our legs under the tank, it wasn't too uncomfortable.

Pete wanted to check how our hiding place looked from outside and climbed back out. When he returned he said that my legs could be seen sticking out from under the tank. We both though it advisable to use the rubbish compartment for hiding. We took our things and climbed into it. This was really grand! It was strange we had not chosen this place first. The water tank was right in front of it, preventing anyone from looking directly down into the room. Anyone wishing to inspect this rubbish room had first to climb over the bulkhead of the chain case, walk carefully over a huge heap of oiled and rusty anchor chain, and then look down into the rubbish room. And as the space between the bulkhead and the ceiling was small, a watchman would have to be very keen and conscientious to bother to inspect our hiding place that carefully. When we found a piece of old tarpaulin and some rolls of chicken netting, we were very pleased indeed. All we needed was to push the rolls aside, crawl in between and allow them to roll back into place. The part of us which was not covered could be hidden by the tarpaulin. To make the camouflage perfect we placed some pieces of old boards on top of the tarpaulin.

This was all fine, but one unpleasant thing remained. We did not know when a possible inspection of the ship would take place, and our position under the net and tarpaulin was most uncomfortable. It was impossible to remain there for more than forty-five minutes at a time. We therefore rehearsed getting everything in place as quickly as possible and in between times stretched our limbs and walked about for a few minutes.

The hours passed very slowly. Suddenly the hatchway was opened. Luckily we happened to be 'down' just then. Several seconds passed without anything happening. Then we heard someone say, 'Hello there – you can come up for a bit.'

We did not answer as the voice was unfamiliar to us. Someone stood listening near the ladder. Then we heard someone climbing over the bulkheads and shortly afterwards heard our Swedish friend's voice right over us: 'You can come up now and get some food and stretch your legs.'

We got up and thanked him. He said we were very well hidden. We had no objection to coming up as we had already been cooped up for twenty-four hours in the cold and damp down there.

The Swede's room mate, a new man, was sitting in the cabin when we arrived. We must have looked at the new man with suspicion because the other two reassured us he would keep mum. For some reason or other we seemed to amuse them very much, and soon found out what it was when they asked us to look at ourselves in the mirror. We were black all over with oil and dirt. They gave us as much food and beer as we could get down, and a large parcel of food to take down with us. It was a welcome interlude, but the time for inspection drew near and we had once more to climb down to our hiding place. Our good friend promised to warn us by knocking five times when the German police arrived. He wished us luck and we were once more left to ourselves.

We climbed down in between the rolls of wire netting and under the tarpaulin and planks. Then waited again, hour after hour. My limbs ached and we got up to stretch our legs. We were anxious and lay down again after a few minutes. Before our camouflage was in place we heard our friend start knocking his signal.

We got down quickly. Counted the knocks. Five! The echo of the last knock had scarcely died away when we heard footsteps over our heads, back and forth. We checked our camouflage once again, for the last time.

Some fifteen minutes passed. We heard the hatch open and someone coming down the ladder. Voices. German voices. Now we heard the German say: 'Was ist da?' A loud, angry voice. And we heard our friend answer – 'Nothing.' The German mumbled, 'Na, Ich will nach sehen.' After that we heard him climbing over the bulkhead to the chain case. All we could do was hold our breath. Cold sweat poured off me. I heard him swear under his breath as he crawled over the slippery chain and over to the bulkhead of the rubbish compartment. I heard him breathing and growling as he came nearer. His torch touched the iron bulkhead which separated him from us. Then he bent down and felt something we had over us. I lay between two rolls of netting and suddenly felt his hand on my shoulder. I held my breath, tried not to tremble, and was sure he could hear my heart beating. Then he let go with a 'Na gut.' And the light disappeared.

I heard him climb back over the chain and soon afterwards they both went up the ladder again. The hatch was closed and we thought we were alone once more, but could not be quite certain, so waited a while before whispering to one another and discussing what to do next. We agreed to lie low for some time yet, because the Swede had told us that ships had another inspection at the outlet of the harbour.

An hour later we heard the engines working and shortly afterwards the ship started to move. We felt the vibration and heard the water rippling on the sides of the vessel. At last we could relax somewhat and ease up on the camouflage, but were prepared to get down again within a few seconds.

We went through five or six hours in this state of readiness. Then we heard the engines stop. We had no idea where we were. There were two possibilities. Either we had sailed at slow speed and had not got further than Stettin's outer harbour, or we were somewhere on the Swedish coast. The hatch opened and we heard footsteps. We hid quickly, but recognized our friend's voice: we could now come up.

In his cabin we were once again given food and drink and he told us his experience during the inspection, after we had told him our story. He had of course been prepared that the German would want to go down to the room under the hatch, and had not tried to prevent him. Had he done so it would only have aroused his suspicions. He had taken a large iron tool from his cabin before climbing down the ladder after the German. The fellow lit up the room and at once asked what was behind the bulkheads of the chain case. Then he climbed over.

'I stood ready to hit him on the head with the tool,' said our friend. 'If he had discovered you he would have got such a smack on the head that he would remember it forever.'

'Or forget completely,' we laughed. We peeped out of the porthole and saw light.

'Light!' – 'Lots of light!' Sweden!

But there was still a long way to Gothenburg, and we had to hide down below once more. Even though we were now in Swedish waters we could not trust the captain. Provisioned with food and beer, we crept back to our hole again and sat comfortably and peacefully on the rolls of netting.

Now we could figure out how best to go ashore. There were two possibilities. Either we could give ourselves up to the Swedish police, or we could try to slip through the police guard and report directly to the British consulate. We decided on the second course, although there would be several technical difficulties connected with it. We could avoid police inspection either by climbing over the fence or by using false papers. This we had to discuss with our helpers. Anyhow we felt quite safe. We were now on neutral territory. Once the boat was anchored at the quay in Gothenburg it would take a lot to get us back to Germany.

The ship's engine slowed down and then idled. Now we were docking. After some minutes the engines started to reverse, and we felt the jerk as we put in. Our friend came down to take us up to his cabin. He and his friend were already in their best clothes and ready to go ashore. We asked their advice what to do and all agreed it was best to contact the British consulate as soon as possible, before the customs inspector came aboard. As we had to pass the Swedish harbour police our friends procured papers belonging to two others.

We washed and tried our best to brush our clothes. They looked extremely shabby after our stay in the bow. Then we went on deck and down the gangway. Swedish ground was under our feet! I felt like shouting with joy but would probably have disturbed the police who were checking our papers. Our friends walked on in front of us. Pete and I followed. This line of action had shown its effectiveness before. Our friends showed their papers. Pete and I were assumed to belong to the same crew and allowed to pass without showing ours. Thus we entered Sweden.

Once out of the harbour gates we hailed a taxi and went into the centre of Gothenburg. We stopped a few hundred metres from our destination, the British consulate, and prepared them by telephone for our visit. We walked at our leisure the rest of the way.

Pete and I did not feel quite safe or at ease until we were well inside the consulate, with a good cup of tea in front of us. We related our story to the Englishman who received us. He made phone calls to a couple of places and then sent us to a hotel for the night. We took leave of our two saviours, the Swedes, and strolled through the quiet town to our hotel.

Next day we were sent to a doctor to be examined and disinfected. Then to the police, to whom we told all we were allowed to. Then back again to the consulate where the consul cross-examined us to be fully convinced of our identity. He found our statements satisfactory and sent us to Stockholm by night train.

An Englishman met us at the train in Stockholm. He was evidently used to receiving people like us, and within a few hours had shown us to our hotel room and bought us new clothes from top to toe, and from the inside out. Then we were taken to the British legation, where we gave a detailed account of our escape.

Since we belonged to the RAF our two Swedish helpers were entitled to the customary reward, which the British official promised to attend to.

A few days were spent writing reports and answering questions. Then our time was our own, while we waited for transport back to Britain. Ten wonderful days we spent in Stockholm.

Then one evening we were told to stand by for departure. We waited at our hotel. Some hours later I was told to report at an office close by. Pete and I had expected to be sent off together. This could only mean that our transport would be by Mosquito, with room for only one passenger. I was taken by car to Bromna airport, together with a British pilot. At the airfield we went directly on board the waiting aircraft.

The flight across Skagerak and the North Sea lasted a little more than three hours. It was pitch dark when we landed in Scotland. I didn't know where we were until I heard two Scottish voices talking in the dark. One couldn't mistake that dialect.

When I got indoors I recognized the RAF station too. I had been there a few times on leave to visit friends before I was shot down.

About an hour later Pete arrived in another Mosquito. Early next morning, 8 April 1944, we went by train to London.

Epilogue

Only when we were on our way across the Atlantic on a troop carrier, on our way to serve as flight instructors in Canada, did we hear the tragic end to the escape we had been part of.

Eighty-two men* had got out through 'Harry' that night before the hole in the ground outside the fence had been discovered and the big alarm went.

Of the eighty-two, seventy-nine were recaptured in various places in Germany and returned to the camp gaol. On account of the large number of escapees involved, the case was taken to the highest authority. Fifty-four of the

---

* There were actually eighty-three men who made it down the shaft: four were caught at the tunnel entrance, three were apprehended at the tunnel exit, which meant seventy-six successfully cleared the tunnel and made their escape. Seventy-three were subsequently captured at various locations, of whom fifty were executed and only twenty-three returned to the camp.

seventy-nine who were recaptured were taken away in lorries one day and shot.

Only three, a Dutchman, Pete and I got back to Britain.*

---

* The Dutchman was Bram van der Stok of RAF 41 Squadron. Müller and Bergsland both returned to Canada and the training wing in Little Norway after they made it to Sweden. Müller's Canadian girlfriend Alice Patricia Tayler, whose letters to Müller were burned by his comrade after he was shot down, had married by the time he returned, and taken the name Trafford. She later wrote a memoir about their relationship. Müller returned to Norway after the war and became a civilian pilot, first for DNL and later for SAS, mostly doing transatlantic flights.